4/13

FANTASY UNDERGROUND

~~How to Draw~~

VAMPIRES

Discover the secrets to drawing, painting, and illustrating immortals of the night

by Mike Butkus and Merrie Destefano

Walter Foster Publishing, Inc.
3 Wrigley, Suite A
Irvine, CA 92618
www.walterfoster.com

This library edition published in 2012 by Walter Foster Publishing, Inc.
Distributed by Black Rabbit Books.
P.O. Box 3263 Mankato, Minnesota 56002

Project Manager: Elizabeth T. Gilbert
Designer: Shelley Baugh
Copyeditor: Rebecca J. Razo
Production Design: Debbie Aiken
Production Management: Lawrence Marquez and Nicole Szawlowski

Printed in Mankato, Minnesota, USA by CG Book Printers, a division of Corporate Graphics.

First Library Edition

Library of Congress Cataloging-in-Publication Data

Butkus, Mike.
  How to draw vampires : discover the secrets to drawing, painting, and illustrating immortals of the night / by Mike Butkus and Merrie Destefano. -- 1st library ed.
      p. cm. -- (Fantasy underground ; fa2L)
   ISBN 978-1-936309-64-1 (hardcover)
  1. Vampires in art. 2. Drawing--Technique. I. Destefano, Merrie, 1954- II. Title. III. Title: Discover the secrets to drawing, painting, and illustrating immortals of the night.
   NC825.V36B88 2011
   743'.87--dc22
                                                                                                  2010052984

022012
17672

9 8 7 6 5 4 3 2

by Mike Butkus and Merrie Destefano
featuring a project by Davin Chea-Butkus

VAMPIRES

How to Draw

FANTASY UNDERGROUND

Contents

Introduction

The vampire is the rock star of monsters.

Beautiful, charming, and supernatural, he can make a woman swoon with a single glance. Today, his likeness can be found between the covers of best-selling books, on hit television series, and in record-breaking movies. Often impervious to sunlight and cast in the role of the romantic lead, he's a far cry from the other monsters in the pack.

But this wasn't always the case. He used to be a loathsome beast who lurked in the shadows, hungering for blood, seeking to welcome victims into his undead Kingdom.

If you've ever hungered to Know more about this immortal creature, you've come to the right place. You've just entered the Fantasy Underground, a land where legends twist and turn like a medieval cobblestone street, a place where monster secrets are revealed in hushed whispers.

In this book, you'll discover everything you ever wanted to Know about the vampire and more. In between sections on folklore and history, you'll learn how to capture these monsters on paper. With step-by-step instructions, you'll find out how to tame this fanged predator through drawing, painting, and computer techniques.

And, if all else fails, you'll also learn how to protect yourself from a vampire attack. After all, this beast may be handsome and suave, but never forget his true mission.

He wants to drink your blood.

Chapter 1: Vampire Basics

Vampire History

The Vampire Controversy

A full moon hovers on the horizon and a crowd of villagers stand around an open grave. A heartbeat passes, and then the coffin lid is pried off. Someone swings a lantern closer, casting beams of light upon the familiar figure that rests inside. An unholy gasp sweeps through the small gathering. The person inside the casket looks like a monster. Skin ruddy and bloated, blood seeping from nose and mouth, even the hair and fingernails have grown longer than when the body was interred.

On top of this, the loss of fluid—a common occurrence after death—has caused the gums to recede, and now the cadaver grins with long, ghoulish teeth.

In an age before embalming, these were all natural signs of decomposition.

But to the Eastern European villagers living in the 1700s, this was surely the mark of a vampire. To these people, this was one of the gruesome undead, a blood-sucking demon that needed to be destroyed.

Surprisingly, this is not the vampire we know today. Over the centuries, this creature has gone from a life-draining monster to a supernatural libertine to a high-school heartthrob. In contemporary literature protagonists now willingly invite vampires home for dinner—even though the tables could be turned at any moment and the hero/heroine devoured. TV shows like *The Vampire Diaries,* movies like *Twilight,* and books like *Interview with the Vampire* portray a modern, compassionate anti-hero who often struggles with guilt-ridden angst over dining on human blood, a pain reminiscent of the plight of the teenage vegan.

Where and when did this change take place?

Until recently, vampires were loathed and feared around the world, sometimes to the point of mass hysteria. People exhumed the bodies of loved ones; they cut off heads and drove iron needles into hearts. They dismembered dead bodies, burned the remains, and then combined the ashes with water. This foul drink was then given to family members in an attempt to halt a vampire's reign. Throughout the 18th century, Eastern Europe suffered from vampire mania, with frequent sightings that caused a near panic. Government officials wrote books and case reports on the subject and, as a result, superstition raged even stronger, causing villagers to dig up more bodies and then stake them.

The 18th-Century Vampire Controversy—as it was later called—got so out of control that the Empress Maria Theresa of Austria finally passed a law against the practice of digging up graves and desecrating the dead. This finally put an end to the madness.

Despite all this, however, the vampire legends continued. Many superstitions were remembered and practiced, whispered tales and so-called sightings kept this mythical beast alive— although the creature was always considered an undead monster. This was the beast of nightmares, not daydreams. Nearly another century would pass before the emergence of our modern vampire—a creature beautiful in shape and form and speech, who now possessed the ability to both charm and seduce. Aptly born in the midst of a worldwide tempest, this new monster would be modeled after a wildly romantic literary figure of epic proportions.

Legends and Myths

In order to fully understand the terrible reign of this undead creature, we must go back thousands of years to discover its true heritage. Known as the mother of all vampires, Lilu or Lilith was born from a twisting series of dark legends. Some claim she was once Adam's first wife; others say she was a Mesopotamian demon. And an early rendition of her with bird talons and wings can be seen on the *Burney Relief,* circa 1950 BC. Later, in the 9th century BC, she resurfaced in the pantheon of Babylonian demonology. Here, she became known as an evil creature who stalked and killed both pregnant women and newborn babes. With a variety of names from Lamia to Kisikil-lilla-ke, her mythical misdeeds were recorded in Sumerian, Akkadian, and Hebrew. Modern authors C.S. Lewis and Neil Gaiman both drew inspiration from her ancient legends. Lewis's White Witch in *The Lion, the Witch, and the Wardrobe* was supposed to be descendant of Lilith, while Gaiman included Lilith as Adam's first wife in his comic book, *The Sandman.*

Moving on to ancient Egypt during the time period of 1400 BC, we hear another early tale of vampiric villainy that centered around the goddess Sekhmet. This warrior goddess, whose cult was so popular that it was moved from Upper Egypt to Lower Egypt, was also known as the ruler over menstruation. One myth states that she once almost destroyed all of humanity, and her bloodlust had to be slated through trickery. The sun god, Ra, convinced her to drink the Nile, which flowed swollen and blood red. The liquid was not blood, however, but a mixture of beer and pomegranate juice—and as a result, her fury was quenched in drunkenness.

Still more vampiric history can be found in Homer's *Odyssey,* which many scholars date between the 9th and 8th century BC. In this epic Greek poem, Odysseus journeyed to the Underworld to seek counsel from the shade—or ghost—of the prophet Tiresias. The hero knew that if he wanted the shade to speak to him, he needed to give it blood from a sacrificial sheep to drink. Before long, however, Odysseus found himself surrounded by shades, all of them craving a drink of the blood that would allow them to speak.

The Revenent

The closest precursor to our modern-day vampire is found in the pre-Christian pagan culture of the Slavic people. With a spirit-based belief system, these people believed that the soul was eternal; they honored household spirits and practiced ancestral worship. They thought spirits could be either benevolent or malevolent and because of this, must be placated before they could do harm. To the Slavs, a soul could amble about after death for 40 days before journeying to the afterlife, during which time it either teased or blessed neighbors and family members. This wayward soul could also re-inhabit its own corpse, becoming a revenant: one of the walking undead who hungered for vengeance and human flesh and blood. Appropriate burial rites were believed to grant peace and absolution to unclean spirits—especially suicide victims, unbaptized infants, and accused witches—thus preventing their desire for revenge against the living.

As these beliefs merged with those of the Romanized sections of Eastern Europe, we saw the inclusion of the *strigoi*, or witches who could turn into vampires after death. Also added to this growing monster repertoire were the gypsy legends from ancient India. Sprinkled among tales of vampiric vetala, pishacha, Prét, and the dark goddess Kali, were rituals for warding off vampires. Here we meet the dhampir, a vampire hunter, himself born of a vampire. Some believed that vampires had the ability to become invisible, but a dhampir was able to see them. As a result of this legend, imposters roamed the Carpathian Mountains, pretending to be dhampirs, staging mock battles for villagers where they warred against these invisible foes. The dhampir may have been the inspiration for Van Helsing in *Dracula*, Blade in *Spider-Man: The Animated Series*, Anita Blake in *Guilty Pleasures*, and Buffy in *Buffy, The Vampire Slayer*.

Human Vampires

Still, not all of our current vampire legends have been built around mythological creatures. Many have been based on the evil deeds committed by humans. Throughout the centuries, many people have walked a labyrinth path of madness and psychopathic behavior, so demented that they have since been labeled vampires. Although these were real historic characters, the line between fact and fiction sometimes blurred over time—partly because the facts were almost too horrific to believe, partly because the legends about them grew with each retelling, and partly because many of the facts were impossible to prove.

The first of these sinister figures was Vlad III, the Prince of Walachia. Also known as Vlad the Impaler, his gruesome legacy inspired Bram Stoker and became the source for the title character in Stoker's celebrated novel, *Dracula*. Born in 1431, his name—Dracula—means "son of the dragon." In 1447, Vlad's father and brother were murdered, and in 1459, he took revenge by arresting and then impaling those responsible, a powerful group of land-owning aristocracy known as boyars. With a reputation of killing more people than Ivan the Terrible, one story of Vlad Dracula claims that an invading Ottoman army turned back when they saw his handiwork: a forest of thousands of impaled corpses that lined the banks of the River Danube. While it's unknown how many people died from Vlad Dracula's sadistic torture methods, estimates range between 40,000 to 80,000.

The second vampiric human ancestor on our list was born in 1560. Countess Elizabeth Báthory lived most of her life in Hungary and later earned the nickname, "The Blood Countess." Báthory and her four accomplices were accused and convicted of torturing and killing 80 young women — although one witness claimed the actual number went as high as 600. In 1610, Báthory's sentence included a bizarre form of house arrest where she was bricked alive into a series of rooms within her own castle. She remained there until she died four years later. Since her death, legends have been told that the countess bathed in the blood of her victims, perhaps hoping it to be a fountain of youth. It is more likely, however, that she committed these crimes out of her own inhuman desires.

The final person who influenced our modern vampire legends was not a mass murderer. He was a dangerously charming nobleman, famous for writing volumes of poetry and infamous for his romantic liaisons with both women and men. Accused of an incestuous relationship with his half-sister and challenged to duels by his critics, his numerous love affairs included English noblewomen and, quite possibly, a 12-year-old Greek girl. If ever there were a model for the handsome and charismatic vampire with the ability to drain the life out of those he met, it was most certainly Lord Byron.

The Romantic Monster

It began in 1816 — during The Year Without a Summer, when world climates plummeted drastically due to volcanic activity in Mount Tabor — as a group of writers and poets gathered in Lake Geneva for a holiday. Included in this literary huddle were Percy Shelley, Mary Godwin (later Mary Shelley), Lord Byron and his personal physician, John Polidori. Kept indoors by the continually dreary weather, they soon grew tired of reading ghost stories and decided to write gothic tales of their own. Birthed from this challenge were Mary Shelley's *Frankenstein* and Byron's "Fragment of a Novel," which later influenced Polidori to pen the first English vampire story. Published in 1819, Polidori's short story, *The Vampyre,* introduced readers to the aristocratic vampire, Lord Ruthven.

This new beast no longer bore a resemblance to the folkloric dark-skinned demon; it had now evolved into a pale-skinned, well-dressed nobleman, both erotic and mesmerizing. Lord Ruthven was fashioned in Lord Byron's image, complete with romantic adventures that echoed the poet's escapades and soul-draining activities. Polidori had used the ancient vampire legends as a metaphor for Byron's depraved, self-indulgent lifestyle.

This new, dark interpretation of the old legends resonated with readers and writers alike and spawned a new genre. *The Vampyre* went on to influence Bram Stoker's *Dracula* and numerous other tales written by authors like Alexander Dumas, Edgar Allan Poe, and Alexis Tolstoy. In recent years, the vampire has gone from romantic literary protagonist to cinematic anti-hero. Now the misunderstood bad-boy-with-a-curse is more popular than ever in characters like Edward Cullen in *Twilight,* Stefan Salvatore in *The Vampire Diaries,* and Bill Compton in *Dead Until Dark.*

It's possible that the vampire frenzy of the 18th century never truly died. It may have simply been waiting in the crypt for that day when the coffin lid would swing open and it would be resurrected by the fresh blood of fans around the world.

In Bram Stoker's 1897 novel, vampire hunter Abraham Van Helsing pursued the legendary Count Dracula. Here, we have pages from Van Helsing's illustrated journal, featuring notes he took when he later traveled around the world, hunting and killing these immortal beasts. He even aptly predicted the twists and turns the vampire evolution would take over the succeeding centuries.

Setting the Stage

Nothing says "vampire" like a moody, gothic setting. Twisted cobblestone streets, cottages with thatched roofs, and flickering gas lamps on street corners: all of these elements help to set the stage for your illustration and will make your immortal monster seem even more real.

15

16

Tools of the Trade

From time immemorial, vampire hunters have stalked the undead. Often led by dhampirs, or half-human/half-vampire trackers, these assassins need the right accoutrements if they hope to succeed. Depending on where the battle will take place, weapons range from holy water and crucifixes to wooden stakes and silver bullets. In some parts of the world, even a vial of poppy seeds or a bag of rice might come in handy—for the vampire would be required to count every grain before continuing his bloody rampage. Since this endeavor could take hours, there's always hope that the sun might rise and finish the task before any more victims lose their lives.

Vampire Evolution

Vampires have changed over the centuries, as legends of these undead creatures spread from one country to the next. From the gypsy folklore that began in the heart of India to the contemporary vampire romance novel, each story leaves its mark on this immortal beast. Once he couldn't survive in sunlight, now it makes him glisten. Once he reveled in his hunt for blood, now he regrets it.

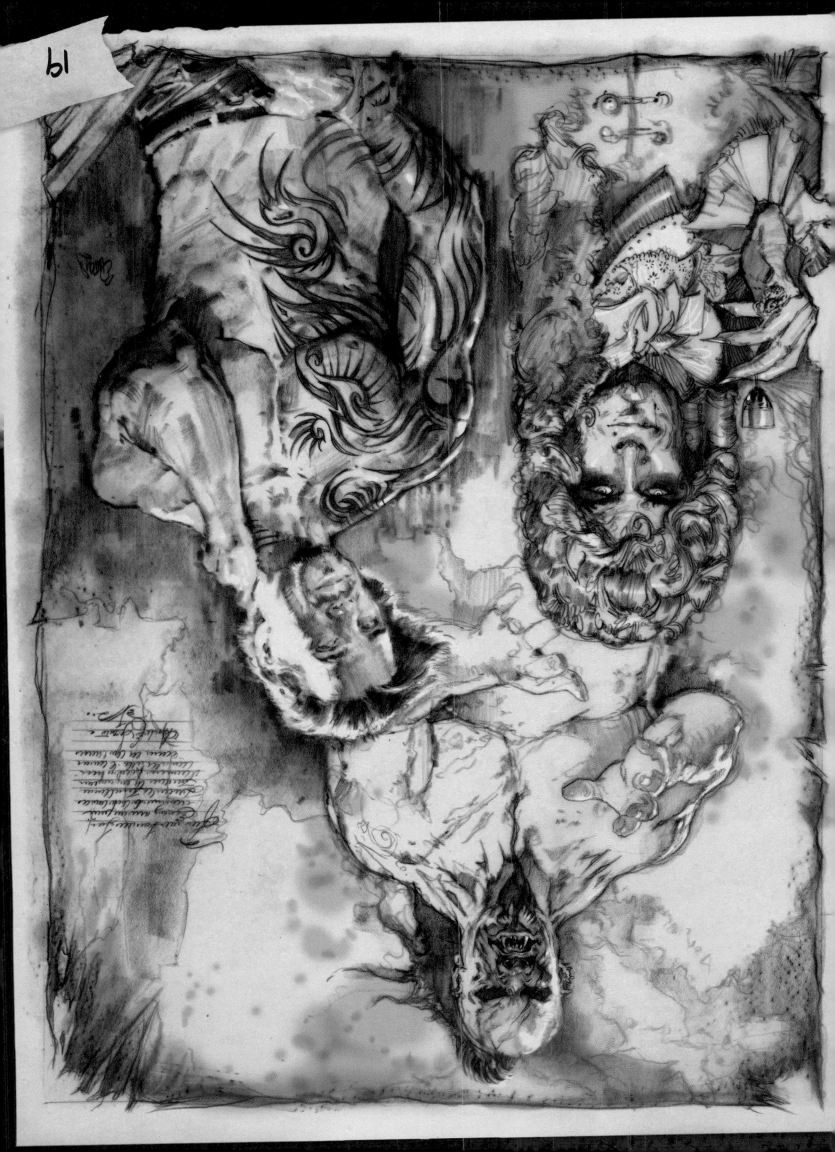

Chapter 2: Drawing Vampires

Drawing Materials

Drawing vampires is a bit simpler than painting or rendering them on the computer, so let's start here. Basically, drawing consists of indicating shapes and defining values (the lightness or darkness of a color or of black). Because one relies so heavily on value to represent the subject, it's important to include a range of values for variety and contrast. Keep this in mind throughout your drawing process—from the beginning stages to the final details.

Black colored pencil

Warm gray colored pencil

Cool gray colored pencil

Small paintbrush

Ruler

Materials Checklist

To complete the drawing projects in this book, you'll need the materials below. Note that the exact materials needed for each subject are listed at the start of each project:

- Multimedia vellum paper
- Black colored pencil
- Warm, 30% gray colored pencil
- Cool, 30% gray colored pencil
- Eraser
- Tracing paper
- Ruler
- Photoshop® (optional)
- White gouache (optional)
- Small paint brush (optional)

Tracing paper

Vellum paper

Eraser

Light Table

The projects in this book will be easier if you
have access to a light table, such as the one
shown on the right. This illuminated surface
makes it possible to create a clean outline from
a sketch, simply by placing a sheet of paper over
your sketch and tracing. If you don't have a light
table, you'll want to keep your initial sketch lines
very light so they can be erased at a later stage.

Pencils

Graphite drawing pencils are generally graphite "leads" encased in wood. The lead comes in grades and
is usually accompanied by a letter ("H" for "hard," or "B" for "soft") and a number (ranging from 2 to
9). The higher the number accompanying the letter, the harder or softer the graphite. (For example, a
9B pencil is extremely soft.) Hard pencils produce a light value and can score the surface of the paper,
whereas softer pencils produce darker values and smudge easily. For this reason, stick to an HB (aka
#2) pencil, which is right in between hard and soft pencils.

In addition to graphite pencils, you will also use a few colored pencils. Colored pencils are less
likely to smear and come in a wide range of colors. (See also "Colored Pencils" on page 71.)

Kneaded Eraser

A kneaded eraser is a helpful tool that can serve as both
an eraser and a drawing tool. It can be molded into any
shape, making it easy to remove graphite from your
drawing surface. To erase, simply press the kneaded eraser
onto your paper and lift. Unlike kneaded erasers, rubber
or vinyl erasers can damage delicate drawing surfaces, and
it's not as easy to be precise.

Paints

The project in this chapter involve mostly drawing, but they
do suggest paint to accent areas here and there. The gouache
(an opaque type of watercolor) and acrylic paints listed are
all water-soluble, so you'll need a jar of water and some
paper towels when using them. You can use either natural
or synthetic hair bristles with gouache paint, but you'll want
to stick with synthetic bristles when using acrylic.

Drawing Surfaces

Traditional drawing paper comes in
three types: hot-press (smooth), cold-
press (textured), and rough. Choose
your texture according to your desired
look. In general, rough paper produces
broken strokes; it's not conducive to
creating detail, but it's ideal for a
sketchy style. Smooth paper allows
for smooth, controlled strokes. In this
chapter, the projects call for vellum
paper, which offer suitable surfaces
for a multimedia drawing approach.

Workable Spray Fixative

Coating your drawings with a layer of spray fixative can help
prevent smudging as you develop your drawings. It's easy
to accidentally smear your strokes. Workable spray fixative
allows you to spray occasionally throughout your drawing
process, so you can prevent accidents along the way.

Vampire Slayer

This provocative vampire slayer found inspiration in a variety of popular sub-cultures, from steampunk to Goth to anime. All aspects of these genres are intriguing, but by blending them together you will create something new and fresh and original. Our slayer stands at the base of a castle, ready to do battle with the hungry vampire queen who lurks inside.

Materials
- Vellum paper
- Black colored pencil
- Warm, 50% gray colored pencil
- Eraser
- Tracing paper

▲ Step One We start this illustration with a block-in using a black colored pencil over tracing paper. Breaking the frame keeps the composition dynamic. The slayer stands in the foreground, while everything else forms a peak that points toward the lair of the deadly vampire queen. (You can transfer this sketch; see "Transferring a Drawing" on page 25.)

Step Two The curling smoke and the full moon behind the castle serve two purposes in this illustration. First, they help set the dark, eerie mood we want to project. Second, they help soften the jagged edges of the castle.

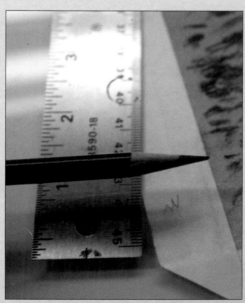

Note: It's extremely important to keep your pencils sharp, especially when drawing at this size and when using vellum paper. It's best to use an electric sharpener that produces very sharp tips (preferably to a 16-degree point). Next, you can use 600-grit sandpaper to further sharpen the pencil. This also creates a chiseled edge which makes it easier to vary the width of your line as you draw.

TRANSFERRING A DRAWING

To begin the projects in this book, you might find it helpful to trace a basic outline of the final piece of art (or one of the early steps). Transferring the outlines of an image to your drawing or painting surface is easier than you may think. The easiest method for this involves transfer paper, which you can buy at your local arts and crafts store. Transfer paper is a thin sheet of paper that is coated on one side with graphite. (You can also create your own version of transfer paper by covering one side of a piece of paper with graphite from a pencil.) Simply follow the steps below.

Step 1 Make a photocopy of the image you would like to transfer and enlarge it to the size of your drawing paper or canvas. Place the transfer paper graphite-side-down over your paper or canvas. Then place your photocopy over the transfer paper and secure them in place with tape.

Step 2 Lightly trace the lines that you would like to transfer onto your drawing or painting surface. When transferring a guide for a drawing project, keep the lines minimal and just indicate the position of each element; you don't want to have to erase too much once you remove the transfer paper.

Step 3 While tracing, occasionally lift the corner of the photocopy to make sure the lines are transferring properly. Continue tracing over the photocopy until all of your lines have been transferred.

▼ **Step Four** In this step, you'll begin tracing in the environment. Considering how much detail will go into this drawing, you'll want to keep it extremely clean. So, use a circle template for the moon and the headlights on the vehicle. Once you do this, you can go back and re-draw them freehand, so they don't look too stiff. Now that the big pieces of the drawing have been laid in, go back and darken your lines, varying them from thick to thin. By doing this, you can indicate depth and perspective while maintaining a dynamic energy.

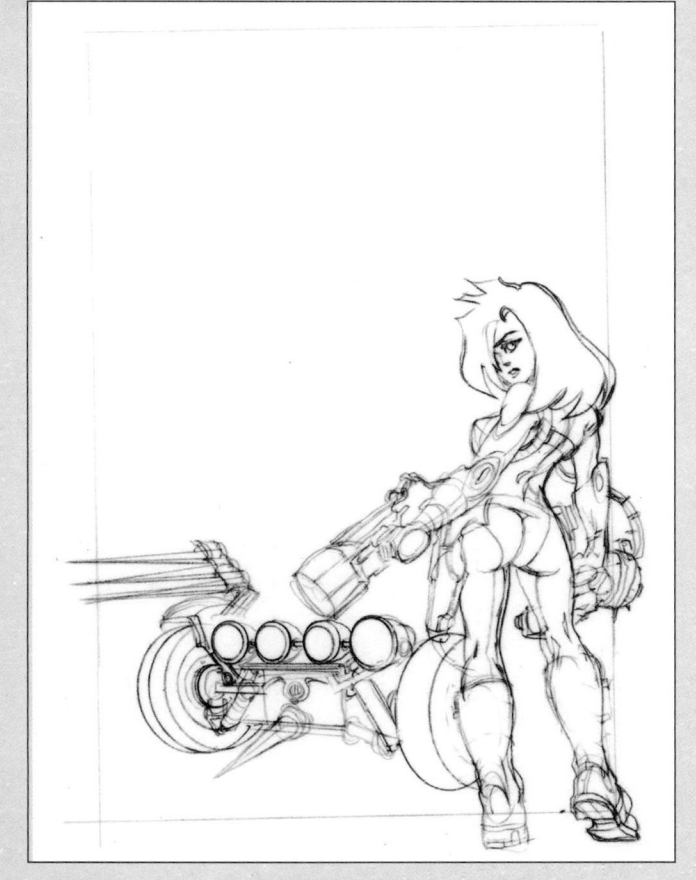

▲ **Step Three** Next, take a sheet of vellum paper and lay it over your rough sketch. Then, trace over your sketch with the aid of a light table, if possible. Try to keep your lines as clean as possible. You may need to change things around a little as you see fit. I enlarged her gun and added even a few more weapons to her collection. Remember to keep both your line quality and shapes varied so the drawing doesn't become stagnant.

◄ **Step Five** Now we'll begin to lay out a whimsical yet Gothic design for the castle, with lines swooping in and out of the architecture. Try to carve interesting positive and negative shapes into the sides of the structure as well. Remember, the shapes that you don't draw are just as important to the overall aesthetics as the ones that you do.

▶ **Step Six** Notice that the bats are flying away from the slayer, leading your eye back to the castle where the dreaded vampire queen waits. Now that the big shapes have been laid in, we can begin adding the smaller details into the castle. With a sharp black colored pencil, draw in lines and shapes that accentuate the curves of the spires and the different castle tiers. Also, expand the base well beyond the frame to add more strength to the structure.

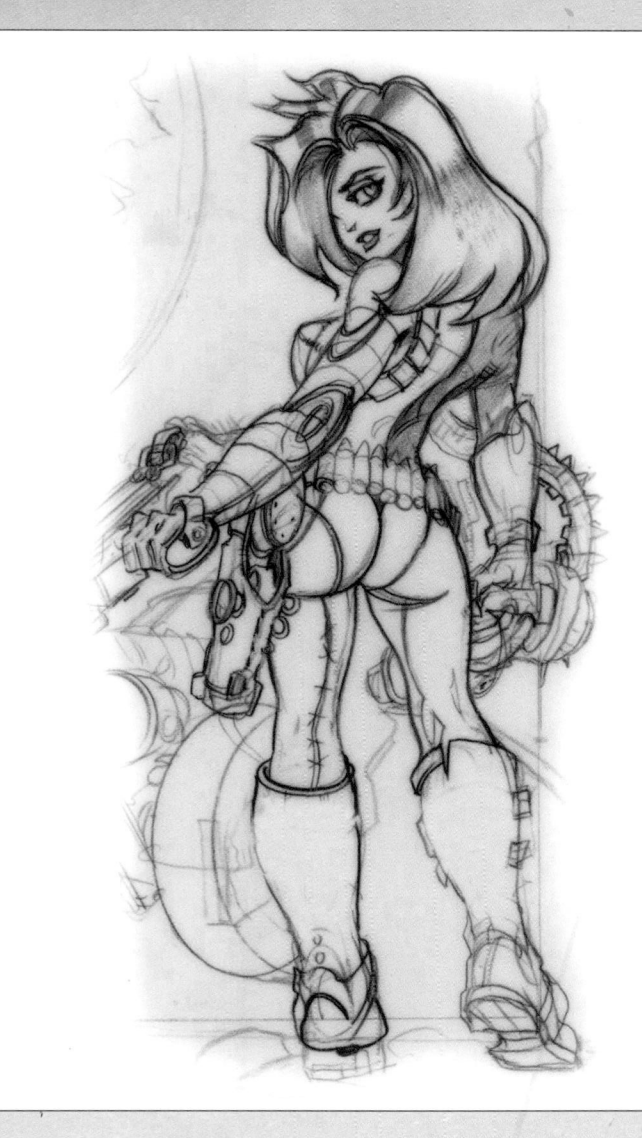

Step Seven Finish outlining the vampire slayer and begin to add some values to her hair and back. Like popular urban fantasy characters, the slayer is sexy but tough. Exaggerate her pose and feminine attributes without making her look ridiculous. Hint at her taut muscles and make her loaded with armaments that only a slayer with superior strength could carry.

Step Eight Here, you'll begin to add all the quirky details to the castle. This is all from imagination but draw your inspiration from both the steampunk and gothic cultures, thus creating ornate gizmos and designs that could run on steam but have a modern flair.

Step Nine It will look like you spent days on the castle but the architecture is actually made from the simple shapes of circles, triangles, squares and so forth. To add more dimension to tiny details, use a warm 50% gray colored pencil and quickly outline the smaller shapes. When creating architecture out of your imagination, keep several things in mind: vary the shapes and lines, maintain a consistent perspective and pick a light source. And have fun!

◀ **Step Ten** In this step, we are going to continue working on the slayer. Focus on her values and make her look a little more 3-dimensional. In contrast to the castle, keep the shapes on the girl round and soft, making her attractive and flirtatious.

◀ **Step Eleven** Next, follow the same technique with the bottom of the castle, varying the lines and shapes. Then, create a small town at the base of the castle, one that lives under the oppressive reign of the vampire queen. At this point, we'll transform the road into one made of cobblestone. This will emphasize the fact that the past, present, and future coexist in this forsaken world.

Step Twelve Now, we're going to slowly build up more tone over the slayer. Exaggerate the twist of her back by giving her right side an overall shadow value. Don't put too much detail into this area since the castle is full of minutia and the drawing needs some clean, big shapes to create balance. Also, at this point, we're going to take another approach with her boots. Since this drawing is inspired by steampunk, make her boots a bit more feminine and incorporate some Victorian touches.

◄ Step Thirteen For the vampire slayer's vehicle, use your knowledge of cars as a reference point, but add a few fantastic embellishments. Keep it low, tough, and utilitarian. Now make her boots a bit frillier and add some more lacing to match the stitching on her back and pant leg.

▲ Step Fourteen We've stepped into a creepy and mysterious world. To convey that atmosphere, make the moon extremely large and use the side of your pencil to shade rings of smoke and clouds around it. Also, add steam to the top edges of the frame and above the small town to create more movement.

▲ Step Fifteen Next, give the slayer's unusual one-sided pants a value of their own. Without the tone, it looks like her skin is stitched up instead of the fabric. To emphasize her voluptuous assets, use a kneaded eraser to pick out the highlights.

▲ Step Sixteen We don't want to bring too much attention to the cobblestones, but they need some texture of their own. Alternate the textures from flat values to dots and strokes, making none of them darker than a medium value. Don't finish the road beyond the frame. This way the edges of the stones frame the drawing. Remember that your border treatment is just as important to your composition as anything else in the image.

Step Seventeen The vampire slayer drawing is now complete.

31

International House of Vampires: Part 1

Most of our current vampire legends have descended from Eastern European folklore. Throughout the centuries, however, many other cultures around the world have believed in mythical creatures with similar characteristics. From an unfulfilled spirit to a dark goddess to a jumbie shape shifter, these ghoulish bogeymen are almost enough to make you want to postpone that holiday abroad.

India

The Bhūta or Prét:

The Bhūta is the spirit of a person who died with his/her wishes unfulfilled; it longs for a human body again. The Hindus believe that these spirits can possess humans and cause sickness, unhappiness, and strange behavior.

The Goddess Kali:

A four-armed Indian goddess, Kali has fangs and wears a necklace made of skulls. She supposedly won a battle against the demon, Raktabija, who was able to regenerate himself from a single drop of his own blood. To prevent this, Kali drained and drank all of his blood without shedding any on the ground.

Scotland

The Baobhan Sith:

This fairy vampire appears as a beautiful woman and often preys on Highland travelers. She has a special penchant for hunters, for they often carry the scent of blood on their clothes. She may also entice a young man to dance with her, and then drain his blood when her prey becomes exhausted from the dance.

Japan

The Nukekubi:

This creatures appears to be human, but has the ability to separate its head and neck from its body. At night, the Nukekubi's head detaches, then flies through the air, screaming and biting human victims.

China

The Chiang-Shih:

A fearful combination of both vampire and zombie, this monstrous beast begins its reign of terror after being raised from the dead. Sporting black fingernails, the Chiang-Shih often has white skin with fuzzy green mold on its flesh. With arms outstretched, this nocturnal being hops about, seeking to drain the life force, or *qì*, from its prey.

Africa

The Asanbosam or Sasanbosam:

This monster dwells in trees and devours its prey with iron teeth. With an appearance similar to humans, the Asanbosam will attack anyone who crosses its path.

The Obayifo:

An Ashanti witch by day, at night this vampiric creature flies about, preying on children. With a strong hunger, this monster is also able to drink the sap from entire crop fields, if desired.

Insatiable

Surrounded by carnage, this vampiric brute has just gorged himself. His feeding frenzy temporarily abated, he stands with a challenging glare and posture as if to say he could easily take on a second village. This project focuses on multiple perspectives and juxtaposing angles, as well as positive and negative shapes.

Materials
- Tracing paper
- Vellum paper
- Black colored pencil

▲ **Step One** We'll begin this project by mapping out a gruesome scene using a black colored pencil on tracing paper. This is the point where you'll figure out how far you want to take this terrifying and gluttonous character. The goal in this illustration is to make it as unsettling as possible. (You can transfer this sketch; see "Transferring a Drawing" on page 25.)

◀ **Step Two** Based on your thumbnail, create a linear drawing on vellum paper. This illustration is going to be tightly rendered, so the approach for the beginning stages will be quite different than those used in the Vampire Slayer on page 24. Map out the dark patterns in the main character's face, leaving his eyes in shadow. Also, lightly draw in the shapes of the light and dark patterns along his body and pants.

34

Step Three Next, begin to draw the background, incorporating a quaint rural village as the setting. Since we are looking up at the main character, his head reaches above the rooftops, making him look larger than life. Another way to make your character more imposing is to make his head much smaller in comparison to his body.

◄ **Step Four** Now, start indicating the hundreds of skulls and dead bodies that resulted from this vampire's insatiable appetite. Make sure they diminish in size as they go back in perspective.

▶ **Step Five** Begin to shade in the values for the vampire's hair and upper body. Be careful to keep your pencil strokes consistent; this will keep your values clean. Add a half-eaten head in one hand the bodies on the street behind him — they looked a bit excessive.

▲ **Step Six** Even though he's got a bit of a gut, you still want him to look strong and fierce. Chisel out his musculature by alternating the direction of your pencil strokes, making him look like he could be made out of granite.

◄ **Step Seven** Begin to block in large dark patterns at the bottom, keeping the values about 15% lighter than their holding line. This grounds the composition, creates a sense of mystery, and reveals attractive shapes at the same time.

▼ **Step Eight** Bow the ground slightly. Make it appear as if it's giving way to the tremendous weight of our hungry vampire and all the carnage he's left behind from his recent meal.

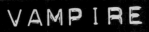

◄ **Step Nine** The bricks and skeletons are used to break the frame, creating a much more dynamic border treatment.

VAMPIRE TRIVIA

QUESTION:
What 1996 TV series, created by John Leekley and Mark Rein-Hagen, was cancelled after eight episodes?
Clues: This FOX science fiction television series starred C. Thomas Howell as a police detective. Howell's character discovered that San Francisco was home to five vampire groups.

ANSWER: Kindred the Embraced

▲ **Step Ten** Start to lay in a mid value for the village. Vary your strokes according to the changing planes of each structure. To keep the feeling of Old World charm, draw all the buildings free-hand, without the aid of a ruler.

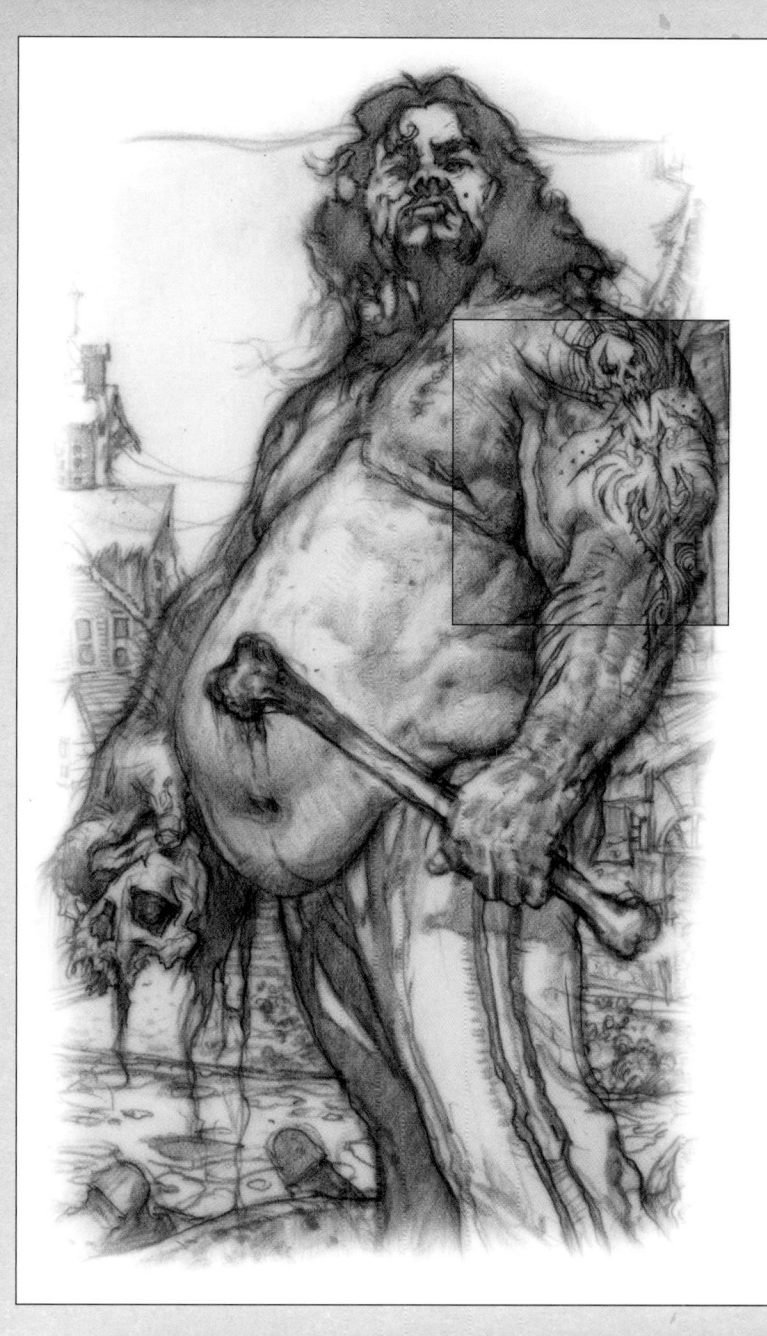

Step Eleven To make him look even more intimidating, design a demonic tattoo for his arm and add a bit of grizzle to his forearm. Push his stomach out by darkening the value along its perimeter. Also, add a shadow pattern on his pants just below his gut, further exaggerating his girth.

Step Twelve Darken your values and holding line a bit more. Since the values in this area are heavily contrasted, make sure your positive and negative shapes are defined and attractive.

39

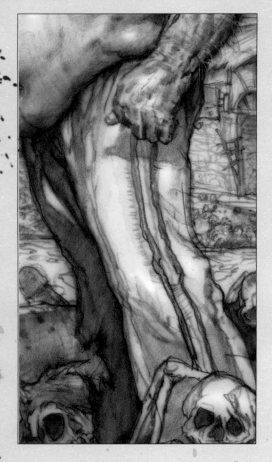

Step Thirteen Yes, this vampire is wearing track pants. This small detail throws the viewer off as to which century this atrocity actually took place. Note how his back leg is enveloped in shadow. In a tightly detailed drawing like this, you'll need to create balance using large, solid shapes. Using graphic shadow patterns will also help add more masculinity to the image.

▲ **Step Fourteen** Is that a pool of blood she's laying in or is that her hair? Leaving certain elements in your drawing unexplained is another great way to rattle your viewer. This dark mass in the bottom corner also helps anchor the composition.

◄ **Step Fifteen** Now, let's take this grisly image a step further. Add a human femur to the clenched fist of his other hand. Make the bone quite long, thus insinuating that the victim it belonged to was no weakling. Add some boils up and down the side of his stomach by lightly shading soft circles.

◄ **Step Sixteen** This ghoul's head is made up of dark and light shapes. By outlining all the shapes with a slightly darker line, you can create graphic forms while still leaving much to mystery.

Step Seventeen Aside from the uncomfortable subject matter, this illustration is an example of many things. In the environment, we're showing multiple perspectives and juxtaposing angles. The dead bodies have very little detail but still read well because they're made out of designed positive and negative shapes. The background is a second read; if you look closely, you can see all the bedlam and mayhem this vampire has caused in his recent rampage on the village.

Punky Vampire

With a hint of youthful innocence, this vampire craves the smokin' hot blood of demons. Spunky, offbeat, and quirky, the character in this illustration has definitely not been following in anyone else's footsteps. The position of her body, her clothes, and even the tilt of her head all help to express how unique this vampire is.

Materials

- Vellum paper
- Black colored pencil
- Warm, 30% gray colored pencil
- Eraser
- Tracing paper
- Photoshop® (optional)

▲ **Step One** To create a spunky vampire character, we'll need to give her a quirky yet unsettling pose. In this preliminary sketch, you'll see that she's sitting on her victim's lifeless body. At this point, sketch a rough lay-in using a black colored pencil over a sheet of tracing paper. Her facial expression, plus the positioning of her arms and legs, reveal her eccentric personality. (You can transfer this sketch; see "Transferring a Drawing" on page 25.)

▲ **Step Two** In this step, we'll continue to experiment with the position of the vampire's body. This character's body language tells a lot of the story, so we want to it to be perfect. It's also important to block in your drawing to make sure the anatomy is correct. Her facial expression is extremely important, so you may want to try a variety of looks for the eyes and mouth.

▲ **Step Three** Now, start the final drawing, using a sharp black colored pencil over a sheet of vellum paper. For a quirkier, less aggressive stance, push her arm behind her knee, as in the thumbnail. Then bring her legs forward and exaggerate the foreshortening even more. Give her eyes dark, heavy eyelashes for added mystique.

Step Four We'll begin with the boots since they are in the foreground. The style of the boots will dictate how to approach the rest of her ensemble. By giving them thick buckles, laces, and "fangs" of their own, they look tough and almost alive. The fact that she has two mismatched boots only adds to her eccentricities.

Step Five On to the dead guy. At first glance, he may look like an average Joe, but he's actually a demon — just the kind of meal this kooky vampire goes after. Although hard to obtain, to the discerning vampire, this demon's blood tastes like fine wine. But we don't want too much attention paid to him, so keep his values to a minimum and the edges soft. He should be a second read in this picture, like a piece of furniture in a room.

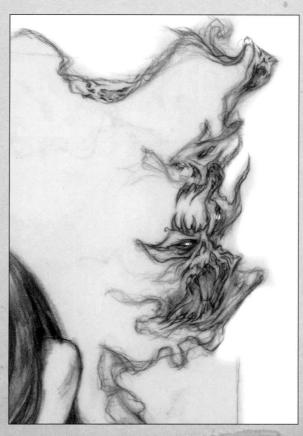

Step Six The framing of an illustration is almost as important as the drawing itself and can add a whole new dimension. The smoke wafting from the bite wounds on the demon is actually his soul escaping. Design monstrous faces within the smoke to represent how abhorrent this soul once was. Make sure to keep the edges soft and the shapes slightly twisted and warped. Note: If you're having trouble drawing believable smoke, try lighting a wad of wet tissue and then observe the smoke coming off of it. The shapes are quite beautiful and graphic.

Step Seven Add tone to the vampire's hair, stroking in the direction of hair growth. Pull out highlights using an eraser. Now we start to add more accoutrements to define this vampire's unique sense of style. While in Europe, I wandered through a wonderful shop that catered to Gothic subculture. I found beautifully crafted ornate jewelry with long chains attached. I tried to design this vampire's jewelry based on those memories, exaggerating them even further.

Step Eight Now, we'll finish laying in the rest our drawing. Keep the folds of material between her legs graphic and strong. Make sure that the lines curve around her thigh to add more dimension. Folds can really weaken a drawing if they don't look realistic. You might want to drape some fabric over a form similar to your subject matter for reference.

▶ **Step Nine** Finish laying in the rest of the drawing, then begin to add your darker values. Lighten up her eyes and darken her skin tone a bit. Also, lengthen her hair, making sure you keep the edges extremely soft.

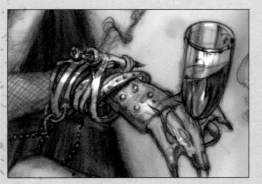

Step Ten Her jewelry is made up of an eclectic mix of metals, so using your eraser (any kind will do), put in some bright highlights down the middle. As for the glass of demon's blood precariously hanging from her fingers, keep the shapes defined and the reflection off the glass bright.

Step Eleven Although this vampire is a terrifying predator to the demons, she has a youthful face — once she retracts her fangs. To achieve this look, keep her features soft and round and even add a few freckles. Give her large doe eyes and a button nose.

Step Twelve In this step, we're going to expand on the idea of the demon's ugly soul. For the background, use a 30% warm gray colored pencil and design a menacing smoky apparition of a skull. Vary the thickness of the line quality and keep the edges firm.

47

▲ **Step Thirteen** By allowing the shapes in the smoke to closely interact with one another, we've created a background woven with intricate details like an elaborate tapestry. In reality, you'll spend very little time on it.

▲ **Step Fourteen** Here, we'll finish putting in all the dark accents and highlights on the boots. To add more character to the shoes, incorporate a variety of textures to the different parts. Also, remember to vary the direction of your pencil strokes, thus adding dimension and weight.

◀ **Step Fifteen** If you want to enhance your drawing digitally, scan the drawing into Photoshop®. Here, we'll darken the overall illustration by about 15% using the "levels" tool (see page 107). You can use the dodge tool or the eraser tool to bring out highlights. Notice that I've isolated her head and tilted it about 15 degrees to her left, adding much more to her offbeat personality. Remember that you have plenty of freedom to experiment once you bring the drawing into Photoshop®.

▶ **Step Sixteen** Here we see the final drawing.

International House of Vampires: Part 2

From the sweltering islands in the Caribbean to the fog-shrouded jungles of South Africa, the vampire continues to make its mark around the world. Sometimes wearing the skin of a human temptress, sometimes pretending to be an abandoned infant, sometimes flying through the night as a demonic snake, its agenda is always the same. It longs to drink your blood.

Haiti
The Loogaroo:
Believed to be a witch who has made an arrangement with the devil, this creature hunts by night, hiding its human skin beneath a silk-cotton tree. Using magical powers, the Loogaroo has been charged with the task of providing the devil with warm blood.

Trinidad
The Soucouyant:
Very similar to the Loogaroo, this jumbie shape shifter is also in league with the devil. She sheds her skin in the evening, hiding it beneath a stone mortar, then flies about, sucking blood. The Soucouyant often appears as a ball of fire and must return, a la Cinderella, before dawn.

Philippines
The Manananggal:
During the day, the Manananggal appears to be a lovely older woman, but at night all hell breaks loose. Her head and entrails detach themselves from her body and she flies through the air with wings like a bat. She dines on the fetuses and blood of pregnant women, feeding with a long hollow tongue.

The Tiyanak:
This babe in the woods is more trouble than it's worth. Believed to have been a human infant that died, this vampire looks like a crying abandoned baby and tricks humans into taking it home. It then attacks when everyone is asleep. The Tiyanak has also been attributed with kidnapping children and getting people lost in the woods.

Malaysia
Langsuir:
Her hunger borne from pain, legends say that this vampire was once a woman whose child died during birth, and then she died soon afterward. Now a demon-like creature bearing long black hair and long fingernails, the Langsuir has the ability to shape shift into an owl. She feeds on the blood of infants.

Colombia
Patasola:

This shape shifter often appears as a beautiful woman and seeks to lure men off into the wilderness. There, she reveals her true desire for human blood and flesh. In its true shape, however, the Patasola is deformed and has only one leg.

Chile
Peuchen:

Just like the run-of-the-mill vampire, this flying snake with shape shifter abilities has a craving for blood. Often attributed with the death of sheep, the Peuchen supposedly has the ability to enchant its victims with just a glance.

Puerto Rico, Mexico
Chupacabra:

The newest monster on the block, the Chupacabra was first sighted in the 1990s in Puerto Rico. Accused of attacking livestock and draining its blood through one or two small holes, this creature has allegedly been seen in areas from Chile to the Carolinas. Descriptions vary from a dog-like beast to a lizard-like creature.

Teen Blood

Falling in love with a teenage vampire presents all sorts of problems. Even walking home from school can be life-threatening. Our modern day romantic hero may seem calm and complacent in the midst of saving his human girlfriend from death, but that's only because he's thinking about bigger things. Like how he's going to explain his latest supernatural feat when all those cell phone photos of the event go viral.

Materials

- Tracing paper
- Vellum
- Black colored pencil
- 30% cool gray colored pencil
- Eraser
- Photoshop® (optional)

▲ **Step One** This black-and-white illustration begins with a thumbnail sketch on tracing paper, using a black colored pencil. We want our teen character to be ultra cool, capable of stopping a big rig with one bare hand. In the thumbnail, work out the body language and the size relationship of the vampire to the smashed truck before starting the final drawing. (You can transfer this sketch; see "Transferring a Drawing" on page 25.)

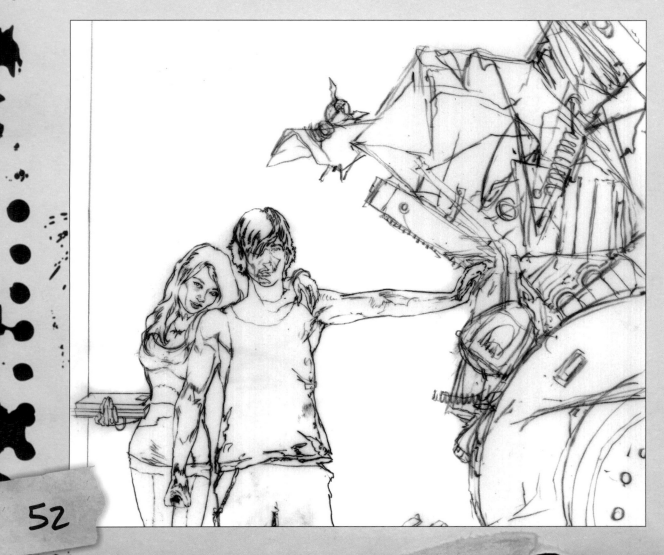

◀ **Step Two** Now we transfer our illustration to vellum paper. At this point, I decided to bring in a cute love interest — a great idea because it adds to the composition and story. However, we still want our teen vampire to be the main character, so keep his girlfriend behind him. Judging from the textbooks in her arms, they were just innocently coming out of school when suddenly a vamp-killing semi attempted to squash the two lovebirds.

Step Three Since this will be a full-valued drawing, you might want to shoot a photo reference. It makes it easier to capture the subtleties of body language when you can get your friends or family to model for you. Map out the character's shadow pattern linearly with a lighter value, referring to your photograph.

Step Four Although we don't know what a truck would look like if a vampire brought it to a "dead" stop, picture it like an accordion folding in upon itself. Have fun with the shapes and include the familiar elements of the truck's front end. Also, make it look like a gaping mouth about to devour the teen lovebirds.

Step Five Next, we'll begin to work on their faces. His is deadpan and unreadable, while hers is demure, confident that her boyfriend will save them yet again.

Step Six Because we mapped out the shadow patterns earlier, it takes almost no time to fill in their values. Keep the edges of the core shadows firm and graphic on the vampire to define his muscles.

54

◄ **Step Seven** Keep the edges on their hair soft and slightly windswept due to the oncoming truck. Make sure that you design the shapes in the hair as well.

Step Eight Next, begin to add details to their clothing. At this point we'll give her a pleated skirt with fun patterns to make her a little cuter. Give his jeans crisp edges to reflect the texture of the material. Also add some dark accents in their clothes to balance out the dark value in her hair.

Step Nine Begin shading in some of the big shapes in the truck. Vary the strokes to add energy to the drawing. Since a lot of this is from your imagination, make sure the dark and light shapes are interesting and are angling in different directions. When making up mechanical objects, be sure to keep the lines crisp and clean and the shapes graphic.

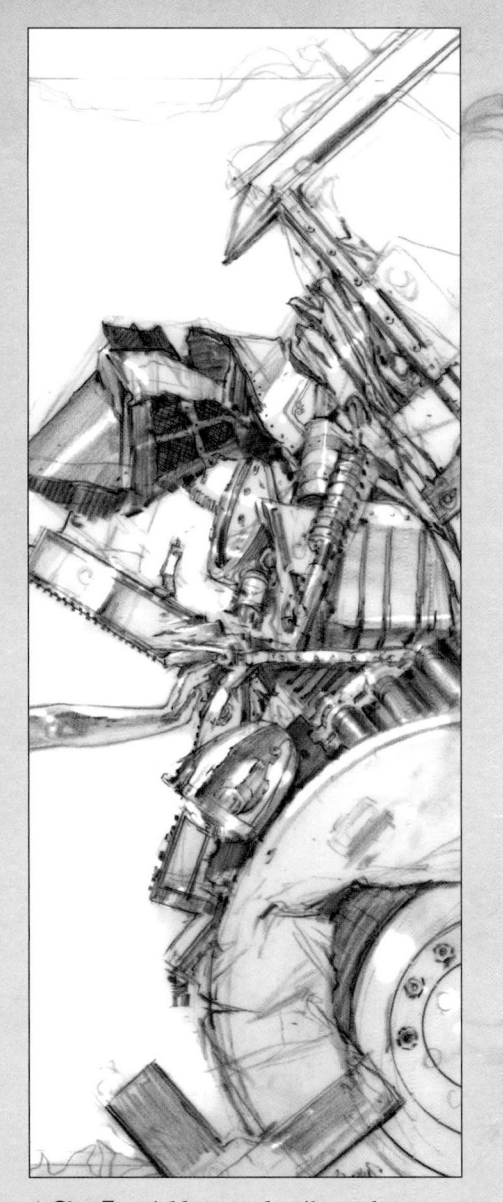

▲ **Step Ten** Add more details to the crumpled truck. Indicate all the nuts and bolts with circular dot patterns. Then add sharp highlights down the middle of all the shapes since they are mostly metal.

▶ **Step Eleven** Lay in a mid value for the rest of the shapes and return to add dark accents. Add more textures to describe the different auto parts. For example, notice the crosshatching on the grills. Using a 30% cool gray colored pencil, draw squiggly lines all around the truck to express the energy and vibration that occur from the impact.

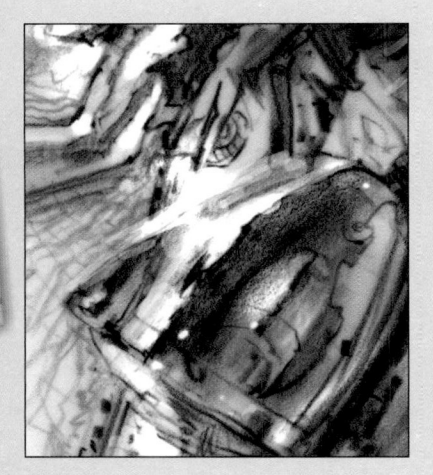

◀ **Step Twelve** When making up reflective chrome, you first need to lay in a mid tone. Then, give it a hard, graphic core shadow that conforms to the shape of the object. After that, put a bright highlight right next to it. If it reflects a busy scene like this, try to design attractive shapes within the shadow areas.

57

▲ Step Thirteen Use the smoke coming off the truck to create a soft border treatment around the image. Also, incorporate the blowing school papers into the frame. Try to make the borders a part of the story as much as possible.

▶ Step Fourteen This girl might be in love with a blood-sucking killer, but she's still just an average teenager. Accessorize her with sparkling jewelry, a floral print shoulder bag, and a bat necklace that declares her love for the vampire. You might want to take note of any teenagers in your family for insight.

Step Fifteen Then, scan your illustration into Photoshop® (see page 107). Here you will create the finishing touches and bright highlights that will make this illustration pop even more. Select the eraser tool, then adjust the diameter to size, decreasing the hardness to about 8% and lowering the opacity. Then darken the background until you have a gray mid tone. This allows you to create bright highlights.

59

▶ **Step Seventeen** Even in the midst of all this turmoil, we still want to infuse some softness and romance to the image. One of the ways to accomplish this is to blow out their hair with soft edges and highlights, still using the eraser tool. Very little time will actually be spent in Photoshop®, since 99% of the drawing has been done traditionally. However, you do not need Photoshop® to complete this illustration.

▶ **Step Eighteen** Here we see the final image.

1920s Vampire

This illustration depicts the nocturnal activity of a vampire in the 1920s. Here we see him lurking about a boardwalk, just before sunrise. Maybe he's heading to a dark hotel room to sleep off a recent kill. Or maybe he's waiting to dine on one of the gangsters delivering an illegal shipment of gin in the background.

Materials
- Tracing paper
- Vellum paper
- Black colored pencil
- Ruler
- Photoshop® (optional)
- White gouache (optional)
- Small paintbrush (optional)

▲ **Step One** This vampire with a hunger for gangster blood lurks around a festive and brightly lit boardwalk. There might have been a prohibition on alcohol in the '20s, but there wasn't any on draining human blood. Our first step begins by creating a light pencil block-in, using a black colored pencil over tracing paper.

◄ **Step Two** Now, we'll begin the final drawing. Transfer your sketch onto a sheet of vellum paper and begin drawing with a sharp black colored pencil. In this step, you can see that I have changed the vampire's look, giving him more personality. The size of his head was increased and now his abnormally long tongue curls out of his mouth. Always remember that you're free to make changes between your thumbnail sketches and your final drawing. (You may choose to transfer the sketch; see page 25.)

◀ **Step Three** It's a good idea to use a ruler when first blocking in a one-point perspective background like this. Once that is done, however, you can do the rest of the background freehand. By leaving the ruler behind at this point, you'll add more energy to your illustration.

▶ **Step Four** The background scene shows a charming, nostalgic boardwalk. Create different-sized shapes for the windows and signage. This adds detail and character to the architecture. Then, fill in the large recessed shapes with a mid value. By designing attractive positive and negative shapes in this small area, you'll achieve a lot of detail work in a short period of time.

◀ **Step Five** You might want to have some reference material on hand when drawing your 1920s delivery trucks. You don't have to be familiar with drawing vehicles, however, to make them look believable. Since they are set at a distance, all you have to do is concentrate on the light and dark shapes, and keep their placement accurate.

◀ **Step Six** Next, we're going to start adding values to our prohibition-era vampire. Make sure to keep your pencil strokes consistent, but vary the direction to describe the form. Also begin to add the dark accents to his face.

▲ **Step Seven** To exaggerate the distance between the vampire and the shops, use a ruler to create crisscrossing patterns for the boardwalk. This also adds more interest to the composition.

VAMPIRE TRIVIA

QUESTION:
What is the title of the 1998 film directed by John Carpenter that starred James Wood as a vampire hunter?
Clues: Since his father was bitten by a vampire, Wood's character roughly fits the profile of a dhampir. On a mission from the Vatican, Wood's quest is to prevent a master vampire from securing an ancient and powerful cross.

ANSWER: Vampires

Step Eight Now we're going to make our vampire even more hideous. Add more warts, darken his gums, and bring down his jowls, making him look extremely well fed.

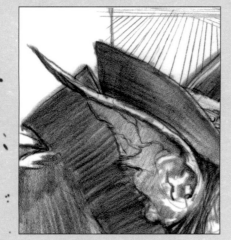

◄ Step Nine
This vampire has been through quite a metamorphosis. Once human, he has now evolved into a bat-like creature. Elongate his ears, making them look like bat wings. Add some veins in his ears, as well.

◄ Step Ten
Pull the skin back from his teeth and give him some gnarly wrinkles along the side of his mouth and nose. By doing this you'll emphasize his grimace.

◄ Step Eleven Once all your values are in place, scan your drawing into Photoshop® and add the final details digitally. Darken the drawing by adjusting the levels (see page 107). Since the majority of the light source is coming from the shops, give the vampire some rim lighting along his hat and his claws using the eraser tool.

◄ Step Twelve Still using the eraser tool, decrease the brush size and increase the opacity. Zoom in on the shops; then quickly add bright twinkle lights along all the signage and the headlights on the trucks. In the background of this illustration, you'll see gangsters unloading illegal spirits. Who knows, these could be our vampire's next victims. It always helps to embed a story in your illustration.

Step Thirteen The last adjustment involves lightening up the sky a bit to show that the sun is starting to rise. Select the eraser tool again and increase the brush size; then dramatically lower the opacity. Next, lighten the sky by about 10%. This digital stage of the drawing (steps eleven, twelve, and thirteen) takes very little time since the majority of the work is already done. If you do not want to use Photoshop®, you can also take a little bit of white gouache (very opaque watercolor) and a small brush to paint the highlights. This will give you the same effect.

Chapter 3: Painting Vampires

Painting Materials

Painting is generally more difficult than drawing because, in addition to strokes and values, you must also consider color and its many aspects—saturation, hue, paint mixing, color schemes, etc. By following the projects in this chapter step by step, you will get ideas for how to approach color and develop your paintings. The focus of this chapter will be on the painting aspect; however, as in Chapter 2, you will have the option of finishing the paintings with a few digital tweaks.

Toothbrush

Acrylic paints

Drawing pencil

Paint palette

Materials Checklist

To complete the painting projects in this book, you'll need to purchase the materials below. Note that the exact materials needed for each subject are listed at the start of each project:

- Acrylic paints: Naphthol red light, Mars black, burnt umber, cerulean blue hue, cadmium red light, cadmium red deep hue, titanium white, phthalocyanine (or phthalo) blue, portrait pink, turquoise, Turner's yellow, alizarin crimson, raw sienna, yellow ochre, ultramarine blue
- Oil paints: Titanium white, lemon yellow, cadmium yellow, yellow ochre, cadmium orange, cadmium red, alizarin crimson, viridian, ultramarine, Mars black
- Assortment of colored pencils
- Eraser
- Electric pencil sharpener
- White gesso
- Matte medium
- Linseed oil
- Maulstick (to steady the hand while painting small details)
- Turpentine or Turpenoid®
- Multimedia vellum paper
- Index card
- Masonite board
- Linen canvas (18" x 24")
- Palette
- Palette knife
- Palette box
- A variety of small to medium size brushes
- Big house-painting brush
- Paper towels and a cloth rag
- Old toothbrush
- Blow dryer
- Airbrush (optional)
- Projector (optional)
- Photoshop® (optional)

Acrylic and Oil Paint

Acrylic is a fast-drying paint that can be diluted with water, but it becomes water-resistant when dry. You can apply acrylic in thin, diluted layers, or apply it in thick, impasto strokes. Oil paint, however, is not water-soluble, so you will need to purchase turpentine to thin the paint and clean your brushes. Note that only one project calls for oil paints (see page 84), and these can easily be substituted with acrylic paints.

Paintbrushes

When using acrylics, we recommend synthetic hair paintbrushes; however, when using oil paint, we recommend bristle brushes. For the projects in this book, you'll want a variety of sizes, from size 00 (a very small, fine-tip brush) to size 6 (medium). Also consider gathering a variety of bristle shapes. Round brushes have bristles that taper to a point, allowing for a range of stroke sizes. Flat brushes have bristles that are pinched into a squared tip. The flat edge produces thick, uniform lines. In addition to these acrylic brushes, you'll also want a house painting brush—a large paintbrush with coarse bristles. These brushes are perfect for quickly covering the canvas with large washes of color. If you own an airbrush, use this when recommended in the projects, as it produces incredibly soft, realistic gradations that are more difficult to achieve with paintbrushes.

Finding Inspiration

While learning how to draw and paint vampires, it's a good idea to surround yourself with plenty of visual stimulation. An entire corner of my studio is devoted to reference books and props.

Paintbrushes

Colored pencils

Painting Surfaces

You can use acrylic paint on practically any surface, as long as it's not greasy or waxy. However, it's best to paint on either canvas or illustration board coated with a white gesso (a coating used to create an ideal painting surface). When using oils, linen canvas (also coated in gesso) is ideal. Remember that the brighter (or whiter) your painting surface, the more luminous your colors will turn out!

Colored Pencils

Colored pencils aren't just for drawing; they are great tools for adding details to a painting. Working directly over acrylic paint, you can add highlights, intensify shadows, create strands of hair, and more. It's important to purchase the best colored pencils you can afford; higher-quality pencils are softer and have more pigment, giving you smoother, easier coverage.

Vampire Portrait

Imagine an almost ageless vampire from Eastern Europe lurking in the shadows of a Romanian café. This stylish patron of the undead has remained on top of modern fashion, and he's so cool that you almost wonder if he's a rock star. Then you catch a sinister gleam in his eyes, and you realize that the bright red stain around his mouth isn't a brand of punk lipstick. It's blood.

Materials
- Acrylic paints: Naphthol red light, Mars black, burnt umber, cerulean blue hue, cadmium red light, cadmium red deep hue, titanium white, phthalocyanine blue, portrait pink, turquoise, Turner's yellow
- Black colored pencil
- Electric pencil sharpener
- Vellum paper
- Index card
- Masonite board (12" x 16")
- White gesso
- A variety of paintbrushes, from fine-tip to medium in size
- Paper towels
- Old toothbrush
- Airbrush (optional)
- Projector (optional)

▲ **Step One** Every project begins with a sketch or a series of sketches. Here you can see the sketch that was the inspiration for this project.

▶ **Step Two** Begin this project by first creating the drawing, using a sharp black colored pencil on vellum paper. The paper is a bit expensive, but this combination of pencil and paper will give your drawing an unbeatable creamy finish that you won't get with anything else. To convey strength and confidence in this character, take the side of your pencil and make quick graphic strokes to chisel out his features. (You can transfer this sketch; see "Transferring a Drawing" on page 25.)

Step Three We want to make sure that this European vampire has all the masculine attributes that a terrifying male hunter would possess, but include hints of femininity as well. To achieve this, shade the eyelids and give him thick lips. Also, give him an edgy haircut and earrings to show that, although this vampire is several hundred years old, he still stays on top of modern fashion. Before you begin the painting process, make sure you are satisfied with the drawing so that you can use it as a reference point. Note: Keep male catalogues and magazines nearby for reference when inventing this type of character.

Step Four Now, on to the prep work for the painting. Lay your masonite board — chosen because of because of its durable and inflexible quality — on a disposable work surface. Mix together some white gesso, naphthol red light, Mars black, and water; then use a large brush to create a warm gray base color for the painting. This immediately sets the tone and mood for the character.

73

◄ Step Five Once the board is dry, we will project the drawing onto it. Use a black colored pencil for this stage as well. Again, keep it extremely sharp. You might even want to keep a trusty pencil sharpener on the desk corner as a reminder.

▲ Step Six On the other side of the masonite board, keep a copy of your original drawing that you are going to project. This is done so that throughout the projecting process, you can stop from time to time and refer back to it.

► Step Seven Now the drawing has been projected onto the primed masonite board. Remember when we suggested that you keep a copy of the original drawing beside the board? Even with this precaution taken, the jaw line and mouth of the vampire came out quite differently from the original. This could have been caused by distortion of the old projector or by my own judgment. In this case, I felt confident enough to proceed and decided to change it accordingly as I began to paint.

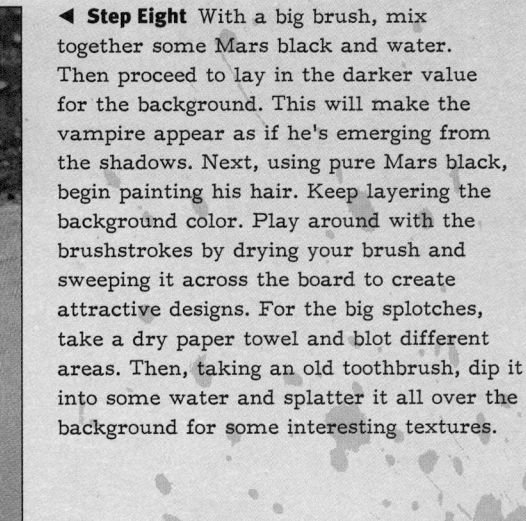

◄ **Step Eight** With a big brush, mix together some Mars black and water. Then proceed to lay in the darker value for the background. This will make the vampire appear as if he's emerging from the shadows. Next, using pure Mars black, begin painting his hair. Keep layering the background color. Play around with the brushstrokes by drying your brush and sweeping it across the board to create attractive designs. For the big splotches, take a dry paper towel and blot different areas. Then, taking an old toothbrush, dip it into some water and splatter it all over the background for some interesting textures.

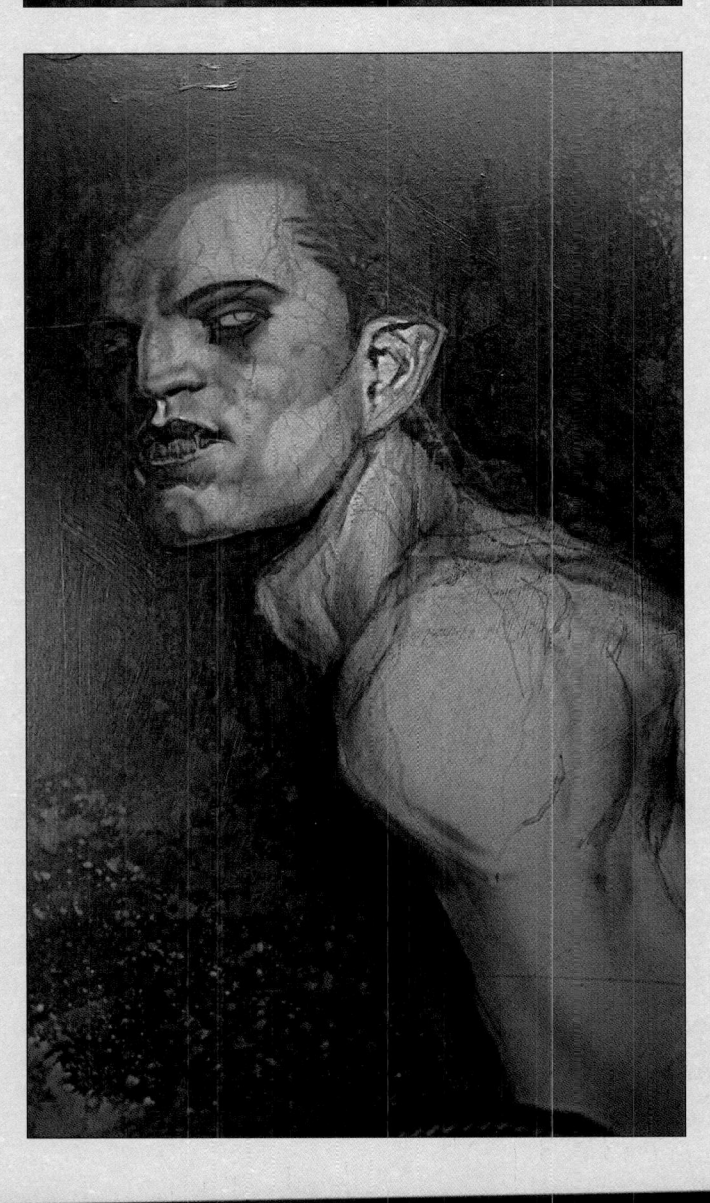

◄ **Step Nine** Now, we'll begin to define the musculature and anatomy of the vampire. If you have an airbrush, fill it with some burnt umber. Then, with one hand, take an index card and hold it about an inch above the area you are working on. Use your other hand to begin airbrushing. This quickly creates chiseled edges for the muscles and soft transitional values at the same time. For example, look at the shadow side of the face. If you don't have an airbrush, build up thin layers of paint, softening edges for a gradated look. Next, for the veins, use a little bit of cerulean blue hue mixed with a good amount of water and start to lightly paint it in with a fine-tip brush. Then, create a mixture of white gesso and a little burnt umber. Use this to layer or airbrush a pale skin tone over the whole figure.

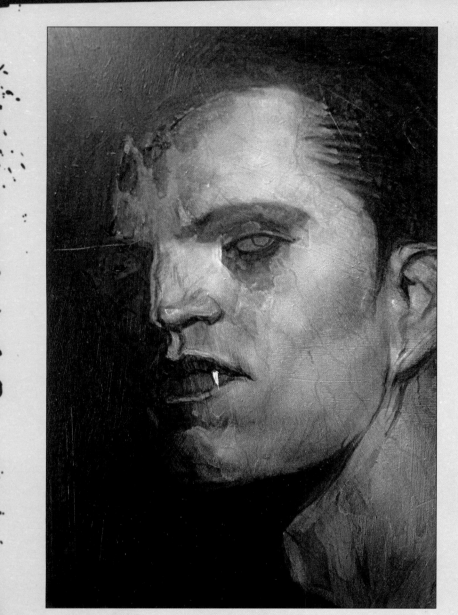

◄ Step Ten For the face, we will begin by laying in the approximate colors that we want for the features. Using the index card technique, start to define the vampire's eyes with a mixture of Mars black and burnt umber. Next, use a fine brush to paint in his lips with a cool red. It looks like he's wearing lipstick, but it's just there to remind you of the blood stains to come. Now flush out the face a bit more. Take a small brush — about a size #2 — and mix some white gesso, cadmium red light, and water. Use this to soften the edges around the eyes, nose, mouth, and ears, adding just a hint of warmth to his face. Of course, at this point you'll also paint in his bright white fang.

▼ Step Eleven Next, add another layer of white gesso and cerulean blue to the face and body using an airbrush or thin layers of paint. When this dries, paint in the veins again and repeat the process. This layering process creates a soft, pale, translucent quality for our undead hunk who, unfortunately, hasn't been able to get a proper tan for the last couple of centuries.

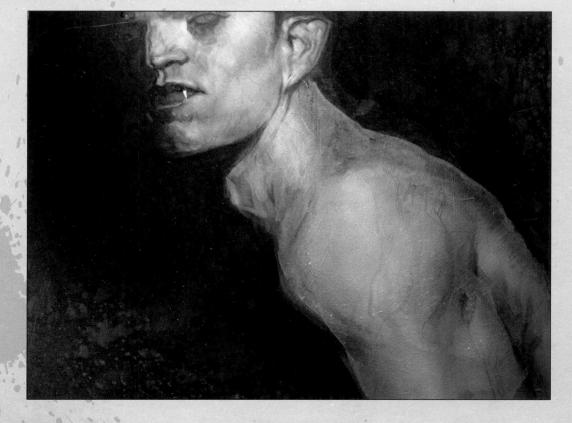

76

Step Twelve We're going to work on the face again, adding some of the more terrifying elements to his features, such as the blood splatter around his mouth and the crimson around his eyes. Using a fine-tip brush, paint some stringy patterns along the side of his chin with diluted cadmium red deep hue. Keep in mind that you need to design the shapes of the trickling blood; keep it attractive so it won't look like an afterthought. For his eyes, begin to experiment with the "look." Mix a little cadmium red deep hue and titanium white. Use this to outline the pupils and the outer rim. Then, with a fine-tip brush, add some highlights for a moist and eerie glow.

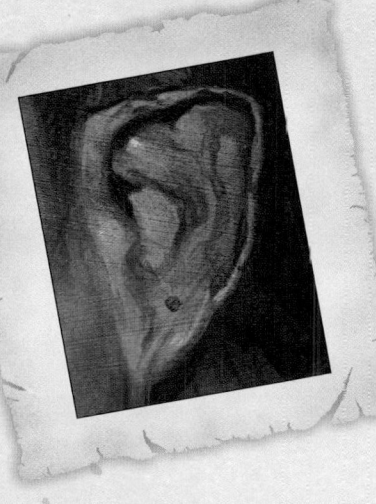

Step Thirteen Since this vampire is a centenarian, we should show that he's experienced quite a few fashion trends. One way to express this is through his hair. Keep the existing background colors and textures for his hair, and just bring in some cool gray-blue strands and highlights to show the style. We want to give him an underground, punk look, while at the same time, the elaborate braid indicates an older history. Also, we'll make the ear slightly pointed. Give his ear blood-red shadows by mixing a bit of cadmium red deep hue and phthalocyanine blue. Keep it uncomplicated, but maintain a play of warm pinks and cool blues.

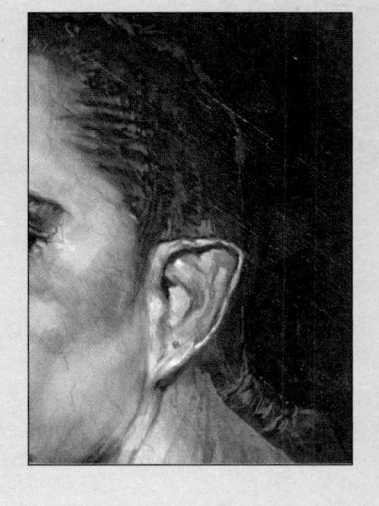

Step Fourteen In this step, layer thin white over the reddish undercolor of the iris for a milkier, creamier effect. Start chiseling and refining his features around the mouth and cheekbone by designing light vein patterns and cool shadows. Also, make him look even bloodier with some wet splattering above the lips and chin. This makes him look as if he's just had a "feeding."

◄ **Step Fifteen** Use a sharp black colored pencil to begin the tattoo on the vampire's arm and back. When designing a large tattoo on a character's body, you must keep in mind the anatomy underneath and make the lines wrap over the structure accordingly. This will help to create a tattoo that is both attractive and believable. Make your shapes interact with one another and remember to vary the line quality.

▶ **Step Sixteen** When you are finished drawing the tattoos, take a small fine-tip brush and begin to paint your designs.

A GRUESOME PALETTE

Here you can see the palette of colors used for the tattoo. You want the colors to be muted yet saturated at the same time. To achieve this, stick with subdued yellows, magentas, and turquoise.

◀ **Step Seventeen** Outline all the shapes with a darker value to accent the graphic quality of tattoos. For this design, symmetry is extremely important. You want the tattoos to appear as if they have evolved and expanded over decades of exposure to different cultures.

▶ **Step Eighteen** Tilt the illustration so your hand can naturally follow the lines of your design. Add more details such as dots weaving in and out of the design, and line patterns at the bottom. Make sure that these lines accentuate the musculature of his arm.

◀ **Step Nineteen** Next, fill in his dark pupil and darken the shadows over the whites of his eyes. Finish the pupil with a dot of blue. Then add more creepy veins all along his face as if the recent "feeding" has made them almost burst from underneath his skin.

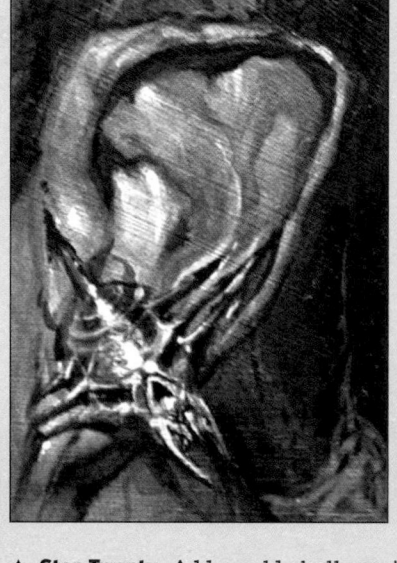

▲ **Step Twenty** Add a gold skull earring as an accessory. Begin by sketching right over the illustration with a black colored pencil. Keep all the edges of the earring sharp; paint some diluted cadmium red deep hue around it. Then, with a little portrait pink and titanium white, brush in thin strips of skin color over the piercing to show the savagery of the handiwork. Paint a little turquoise around the gold to unite it with the coolness of the vampire and, also, to show that this earring is an ancient relic.

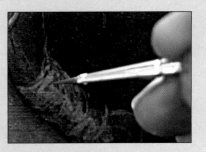

Step Twenty-One Now, on to his hair. We're going to create an ornate gold band for his braid. Quickly lay in a gold tone using a mixture of Turner's yellow and a little phthalocyanine blue. Make sure your brushstrokes follow the form of the hair. Then, paint a highlight down the middle, allowing the values to drop off at the edges.

Step Twenty-Two In this step, we finish off the exotic hair band with a little bit of orange and some bright highlights that indicate the intricate engraving.

Step Twenty-Three The braid is quite simple to do. Just indicate it by using a small brush and paint some highlights along the edges, recreating the silhouette of a braid. When painting his hair, be sure to stroke in the direction of hair growth.

Step Twenty-Four We're going to make the vampire a bit more human-like by defining his iris with warm colors, but still keeping it pale. Make sure that the shadow under the upper lid is the appropriate value so his eye doesn't look flat.

Step Twenty-Five Here we see the completed painting of our vampire.

Protection From a Vampire

What do you do if you're walking down a dark alley in Romania or Transylvania and suddenly find yourself face-to-face with a vampire? The best idea is to just turn around and run. But if that option isn't available, you might want to consider some of the suggestions below. Of course, since the vampire legends differ around the world, your necessary accoutrements will need to differ as well. So, we recommend that you go into that alley like Van Helsing—prepared for survival.

The European Vampire
1. Fill your pockets with garlic; the more, the better.
2. Carry sacred items like holy water, a rosary, or a crucifix.
3. Keep a sprig of wild rose or hawthorn at hand.
4. Hang a mirror on your front door, facing outwards.
5. Don't invite him/her into your house.
6. Don't rely on sunlight to save you. Some vampires are impervious to the sun.
7. Carry a stake, preferably made from oak, hawthorn, or ash.
8. Cut off his/her head. Then run. Just in case he/she has friends nearby.

The Scottish Vampire
1. Beware of anyone with a strange accent and hooves.
2. Carry a weapon made of iron. Better yet, carry two.

The African Vampire
1. Don't offer fruit to anyone with glowing armpits. If fed, the voracious Obayifo may decide to suck the life out of your children and your crops.

The Japanese Vampire
1. Watch out for anyone with red symbols around their neck.
2. Destroy the Nukekubi's body while its head is out on a mischievous errand.

The Chinese Vampire
1. Get thee across water. The Chiang-Shih has a slight problem with running water.
2. Hold your breath. Yes. Really.
3. Carry garlic and salt.
4. Pray for a thunderstorm. Loud noises chase these beasts away.

The Haitian/Trinidad/Philippine/Malaysian Vampire

1. Sprinkle sand or rice outside windows and doors. Both the unsuspecting Loogaroo and the Soucouyant will be forced to stop and count every grain before attacking.
2. Sprinkle salt on the skin left behind when the Soucouyant shape shifts.
3. Hang a variety of garlic, onion, and thistle branches around your windows and doors to prevent the Manananggal or Penanggalan from entering.
4. Turn your clothes inside out. Apparently this bizarre behavior amuses the Tiyanak so much that it will set you free.
5. Cut her hair and fingernails. Then stuff them into that convenient hole in the back of her neck. This will make a Langsuir turn into a human woman.

The South American/Mexican Vampire

1. Beware of one-legged beautiful women who try to befriend you in the wilderness.
2. Consult with the Machupe medicine woman. She's got the inside scoop on how to get rid of that enormous flying snake that's been following you.
3. Avoid that strange dog-like creature with glowing eyes that has the ability to hypnotize. He's not your new best friend.

WHEN ALL ELSE FAILS

Sometimes prevention is the best solution. In these cases, you need to strike first.

1. Find the vampire's grave. You'll need to walk through the cemetery, followed by a virgin stallion whose rider is a virgin boy. The horse will let you know which grave is suspicious. Or he may just let you know that he's tired of gallivanting about through the graveyard.
2. Place iron needles in the sleeping vampire's heart and mouth. The trick is to make sure he stays asleep throughout the process.
3. Put hawthorn in the vampire's sock.
4. Douse the vampire's grave with boiling water.
5. Place garlic in the vampire's mouth. Perhaps you could serve it up with some pasta and a green salad.
6. Cut up the vampire's corpse, and then burn it. Wait. You're not done. Mix with water. Still not done. Now serve this foul liquid to family members who have been tormented by the vampire. That should stop their whining and complaining.

Lady V *by Davin Chea-Butkus*

You never know who might wander into your studio and want a portrait painted. In this case, it was a wealthy vampire socialite—known to all the elite bluebloods as Lady V. You'll notice that she wasn't able to make it through the sitting without a snack. Make sure any potential undead clients understand that you are not on the menu.

Materials

- Oil paints: Titanium white, lemon yellow, cadmium yellow, yellow ochre, cadmium orange, cadmium red, alizarin crimson, viridian, ultramarine, Mars black
- Linen canvas (18" x 24")
- Palette
- Palette knife
- A wide variety of bristle brushes
- Linseed oil
- Maulstick (to steady the hand while painting small details)
- Turpentine or Turpenoid®

Step One Before you start painting, lay out your colors beginning with white and then moving on to warm and cool colors. Make sure you have a variety of brush sizes available and plenty of room to mix your paint.

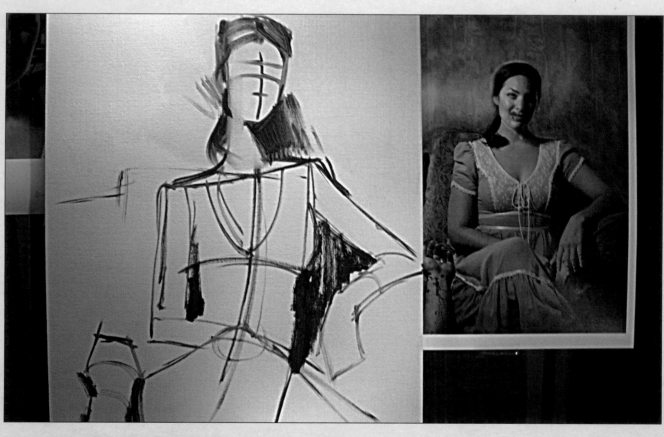

Step Two One common element in most formal portraits is the display of the sitter's most prized belongings. In this vampire socialite's case, her pride and joy is a fresh kill. Begin your block-in using a mixture of alizarin crimson, yellow ochre, and viridian. This will create a mid value — neither too warm nor too cool — that won't interfere with subsequent layers of paint. Notice that I work with my photo reference within view. (You may choose to transfer the sketch for this project; see "Transferring a Drawing" on page 25.)

Step Three Looking at the photo reference, you'll notice that the left side of the model's face is in bright light, transitioning to warm shadows on the right. When working on the color block-ins, try to create big blocks of accurate color, value, and temperature right away. You can also develop the background and foreground at the same time, so the white canvas won't be a distraction.

Step Four Next, quickly lay in large shapes of color for the shadows and the lights. Step back frequently to make sure your proportions have remained intact.

◄ **Step Five** The wonderful thing about using a spacious palette is that you'll be able to see and compare all the colors you've mixed. Then you can quickly dip into the mixture you need, whether it be for the skin tone, the dress, or the background.

◄ **Step Six** In this step, you'll cover the rest of the canvas and with broad strokes. Paint in the direction that best describes that particular form. In this early stage, one of your main concerns will be establishing the light and dark patterns.

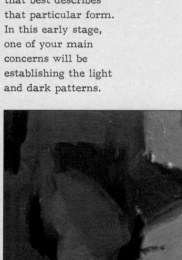

▲ **Step Seven** You want to establish right off the bat that the victim's hand belongs to a big, burly guy. Once again, this proves that size does not matter in a battle with the undead.

Step Eight Now, start on the face. Squint at your photo reference to see the graphic shapes of the light and dark patterns; then begin painting these shapes.

▲ Step Nine First, concentrate on the eyes. It's extremely important to keep the edges soft and the colors clean when painting the eyes. By doing this, you'll bring life and vitality to the painting.

▶ Step Ten Once the eye is laid in, move on to the rest of the face. Again, remind yourself to keep the edges soft. Step away from the canvas often to make sure the features are not misaligned. Another technique for monitoring proportion and placement involves looking at the reflection of your painting through a mirror. You will spot any mistakes right away.

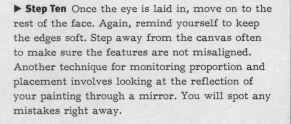

◀ Step Eleven Since this vampire fed right before her sitting, we want her to look slightly flushed with exhilaration. Mix a little bit of alizarin crimson, a bit of yellow ochre, and some white; then use this to paint the blush on her right cheek and nose. Also, make sure to observe all the little highlights on her face and even exaggerate them slightly to give her a healthy glow.

◀ **Step Twelve** At this point, we'll work on the background, making it a subdued grayish blue with a little interest in it as well. Take your palette knife, then scrape off some paint in certain areas. This will reveal a bit of the underlying colors while adding texture.

▲ **Step Thirteen** Continue looking for errors in proportion. In this case, I noticed that her head was becoming a bit large, so I broadened her shoulders a bit by extending the sleeves. Start to bring in the shadows along the side of her torso and the bottom of her dress. Keep the shapes graphic to uphold the structure.

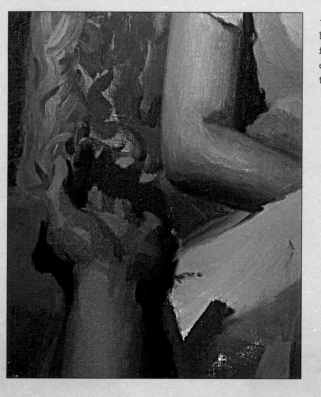

◄ **Step Fourteen** Here, we begin to refine the shadowy side of her face and soften all of the edges. We also paint in the long-awaited fangs. Leave a light smear of blood on one corner of her mouth, as if she missed wiping it off with her handkerchief.

▼ **Step Fifteen** Since the upholstery is not our main focus, we don't have to spend a lot of time copying the patterns. Approach it the same way you did with the vampire. First, block in the big shapes of color and value. Then, subtly indicate the floral pattern with a smaller brush. Paint it as if you're looking at the sofa while standing 10 feet away.

◄ **Step Sixteen** Hands are often thought of as being very difficult to paint because of all the fingers, knuckles, and so forth. Ignore these elements and just focus on one big shape at a time, gradually moving to the smaller ones.

▲ Step Seventeen Use the same approach as you did in Step Sixteen when working on the lady vampire's hand. But this time you want it to look long, delicate, and slender, in contrast to the hand of her victim.

▼ Step Eighteen Her dress is made up of beautiful shades of lilac and blues. When hit by the light, there's a hint of transparency. To achieve this look, mix a bit of cadmium orange, ultramarine blue, and white. Then, apply this between the folds of her sleeves, along the side of her bodice, and over her crossed leg.

▲ Step Nineteen For the lace embroidery, mix a batch of warm white and cool white. Then, use a small brush and begin to indicate the little flowers with small quick strokes. Make sure to adjust the white as you move into the shadow area.

◄ Step Twenty Hair is another area where the edges need to be soft. Do this by observing the transition of colors and values — not by blending.

91

▲ **Step Twenty-One** Finish the hand, and then move on to the blood and gore. Since we don't have a reference for the gore, we won't spend too much time trying to make it up — otherwise the gore could end up looking unbelievable. Mix a little cadmium red and alizarin crimson for the smudges of blood. Then mix alizarin crimson and ultramarine blue for the puncture wounds. Also add some bruising for more realism.

▶ **Step Twenty-Two** Once you are done, take a few steps back and study the painting for anything you may have overlooked. It's easier to fine-tune your oil painting during the first couple of days after it's finished, when the paint is still wet and malleable.

Bounty Hunter

This vampire bounty hunter hikes through snow and a barren landscape, with nothing but a vicious wolf and an arsenal of weapons for company. And yet, despite her gruesome task, few vampires have been able to resist her when she draws near. This project will give you the opportunity to work with a model and a photo reference, thus creating a more realistic drawing.

Materials
- Acrylic paints: Alizarin crimson, raw sienna, yellow ochre, ultramarine blue, burnt umber
- Palette box
- Matte medium
- Large house painting brush
- Masonite board
- Assortment of small acrylic paintbrushes
- Vellum paper
- Assortment of colored pencils
- Eraser
- Airbrush
- Photoshop®
- Blowdryer

▲ **Step One** This illustration is more realistic and aims to capture all the subtle nuances of the human figure. So, you may need to set up a photo shoot with an appropriate model. (However, finding a psychotic wolf to pose for you may prove difficult.) Create an initial sketch that defines the shapes and maps the shadow patterns. (You can also transfer the sketch from this book; see "Transferring a Drawing" on page 25.)

▶ **Step Two** Notice that as I develop the sketch, I get rid of the spiky cuffs on her wrists and the spikes on the sword. These shapes are too distracting to the viewer. Also, I push her left hip out a bit further so she'll have a more relaxed demeanor. It's important to take some time to think through and refine your sketch. Edit her costume a bit more, then work on the wolf, exaggerating his demonic expression.

▶ Step Three Once you're happy with her body language, begin shading in the darks. Use light, consistent strokes for the shadow patterns. Heavy handedness can detract from the femininity of a female figure.

▲ Step Four Slowly darken the values, keeping the edges soft. At this point, we're getting a better feel for what her gear should look like. Make the design of the weapons feminine, yet still keep dangerous razor-sharp edges. Even the nastiest vampire would think twice about resisting capture by this bounty hunter.

95

◀ **Step Five** Our bounty hunter is trekking through the snow, so she needs more practical boots for this mission. Give her boots that are made with tough leather, have thick soles, and are equipped for carrying multiple silver daggers.

▲ **Step Six** Her silver body armor makes graphic light and dark patterns, so let's brighten up the highlights even more. Also, begin shading in the wolf. He's barely able to contain his frenzy for vampire blood, so convey this with quick pencil strokes, creating fur that seems to shoot from his body.

▶ **Step Nine** Once you're done with the drawing, begin to prep it for painting. You'll need a warm undertone for this painting, and there are a few ways to quickly achieve this. You can either take your drawing and run it through a color copier, selecting the "sepia tone" setting. Or if you have Photoshop®, scan it in and adjust the color balance to your liking. You may also complete this stage traditionally by sealing (see Step Eleven on page 98) and toning the drawing with a warm wash of paint. However, using the shortcuts described above will produce similar results.

▶ **Step Seven** Continue using frenetic pencil strokes for the rest of the wolf's body. Then, add dark accents along his ears and in his gaping mouth, leaving his fangs bright white. The combination of his raised fur and the crosshatching strokes in between give a maniacal energy to this not-so-cuddly beast.

▶ **Step Eight** Next, indicate soft shadows and indentations in the snow, thereby grounding the characters. Also, add a scenic background of pine trees in the distance.

◄ Step Ten While we're in Photoshop®, let's brighten up the highlights (see page 107). Select the eraser tool, then lower the opacity to about 15% and change the mode to "multiply." Then, slowly brighten up the areas along her stomach, her armor, and the snow. Create the moon with the dodge tool and select a warm, off-white color from the palette. Increase the opacity to about 75% for the moon's center, and then decrease it in the same way as the moon's glow.

▼ Step Eleven Next, print out your drawing on regular copy paper. Then, mount it onto a masonite board using a mixture of 50% matte medium and 50% water. Just take any old house brush and use it to slather the matte medium mixture over the print. If desired, you can use a blow dryer to speed up the drying process. Once it dries, the illustration will be sealed and ready for the acrylic paints.

Step Twelve We'll use a limited palette and keep the colors muted for this painting. First, knock the sky back by coating it with a cool value of burnt umber and ultramarine blue. Then, using the same mixture, lightly dust both her skin and the wolf. You can either use an airbrush or apply thin layers of paint.

▲ **Step Fourteen** Her face is set in shadow, so paint it with cool tones. Add a little raw sienna and yellow ochre for warmth in her features. Then, for all the highlights use an extremely sharp cream colored pencil and lightly go over the top planes.

▼ **Step Fifteen** Paint the wolf with warm and cool washes. Since there's no black in our palette, take a black colored pencil and outline his fur and darken the shadow areas. Also, use other colored pencils to detail his fangs and eyes.

▲ **Step Thirteen** Mix a little ultramarine blue, yellow ochre, and a lot of water to create a wash. Then use this to paint in the bounty hunter's sword and silver armor. You want the drawing and the warm undertone to come through, so you'll be doing a lot of layering with the diluted paint. Add some warmth to her skin and her gear by using a little alizarin crimson and yellow ochre.

◄ Step Sixteen Now you can scan the painting into Photoshop® for the finishing touches. Working on the computer to complete a painting gives you the freedom to test out large and daring adjustments without ruining the physical painting.

► Step Seventeen Once in Photoshop®, you can play around with the sky. Darken it, giving it a purple hue. This contrasts nicely with her warm skin tone.

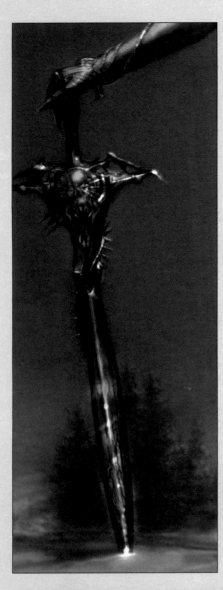

◄ **Step Eighteen** Sample the purple from the sky using the eyedropper tool, and use the brush tool to lightly paint her glove and sword. Use the dodge tool for the highlights, keeping the opacity around 40% so that it will pick up the color underneath.

▶ **Step Nineteen** What is a homicidal wolf without copious amounts of drool? Take the eraser tool, then lower the diameter and keep the opacity at about 50%. Then, simply draw in the disgusting dribble that only the bounty hunter could love.

Step Twenty Darken the shadows in the snow to weigh down the characters. Then, give the snow a softer, slushier texture. Select the eraser tool, decrease the hardness to 0% and the opacity to about 50%, and pull the eraser over the light areas.

▶ **Step Twenty-one** Here we see the final image.

VAMPIRE TRIVIA

QUESTION:
What 2009 film, directed by Paul Weitz, was based on the 12-volume young adult series titled *The Saga of Darren Shan*? Clues: The film tells the tale of a 16-year-old boy named Darren, played by Chris Massoglia, who agrees to become a half-vampire in order to get the antidote to a dangerous spider bite.

ANSWER: *Cirque de Freak: The Vampire's Assistant*

102

Chapter 4:
Vampires &
Digital
Illustration

Digital Illustration Materials

Digital illustration can result in highly detailed, fiercely dynamic artwork. Unlike drawing or painting, digital illustration allows you to make dramatic enhancements with just a few clicks of a button. Before working on the projects in this chapter, note that it's important to have an understanding of the basic tools and functions of your image-editing software (I prefer Photoshop®). However, if you don't have a background in digital illustration, you can still use these projects as references for drawing or painting—each piece of art begins with a drawing or painting by hand.

Paintbrushes

Acrylic paints

Colored pencils

Paint palette

Materials Checklist

To complete the illustration projects in this book, you'll need the materials below. Note that the exact materials needed for each subject are at the start of each project:

- Acrylic paints: Mars black, Payne's gray, viridian hue permanent, turquoise deep, cerulean blue hue, cadmium red light, iridescent antique brown, titanium white, cadmium red deep hue, Turner's yellow, cadmium yellow
- Acrylic paint palette
- Palette box
- Variety of small acrylic brushes
- Large house painting brush
- An assortment of colored pencils (cool, 30% gray; white; and black)
- Tracing paper
- Masonite board (8" x 10")
- Vellum paper
- Workable spray fixative
- Matte medium
- Airbrush (optional)
- Computer system and Photoshop®
- Scanner

Computer System

To embark on your journey in digital illustration, you'll need a computer system, a scanner, and image-editing software. In the setup at right, you'll see that you can configure multiple monitors for one computer system. This can help you spread out your work; you can bleed the monitors so that your image crosses over onto multiple screens, allowing you to see much more of the image at once. You can also use the multiple monitors to hold various control panels, so you aren't constantly minimizing windows to create room on the screen. Although it's ideal to work with several monitors, all you really need is one.

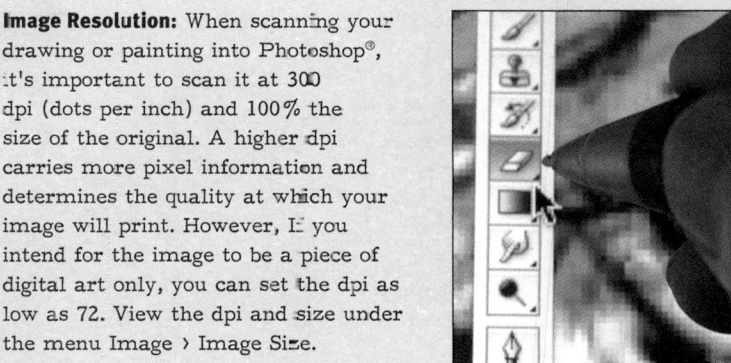

Image-Editing Software

There is a variety of image-editing software available, but many would agree that Adobe® Photoshop® is the most widely used. Below are short summaries of some basic functions used in the projects throughout this book.

Photoshop® Basics

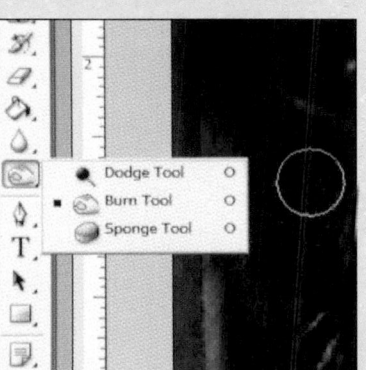

Image Resolution: When scanning your drawing or painting into Photoshop®, it's important to scan it at 300 dpi (dots per inch) and 100% the size of the original. A higher dpi carries more pixel information and determines the quality at which your image will print. However, if you intend for the image to be a piece of digital art only, you can set the dpi as low as 72. View the dpi and size under the menu Image > Image Size.

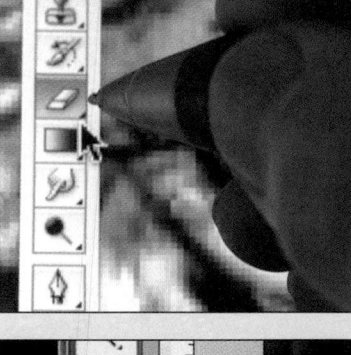

Eraser Tool: The eraser tool is found in the basic tool bar. When working on a background layer, the tool removes pixels to reveal a white background. You can adjust the diameter and opacity of the brush to control the width and strength of the eraser.

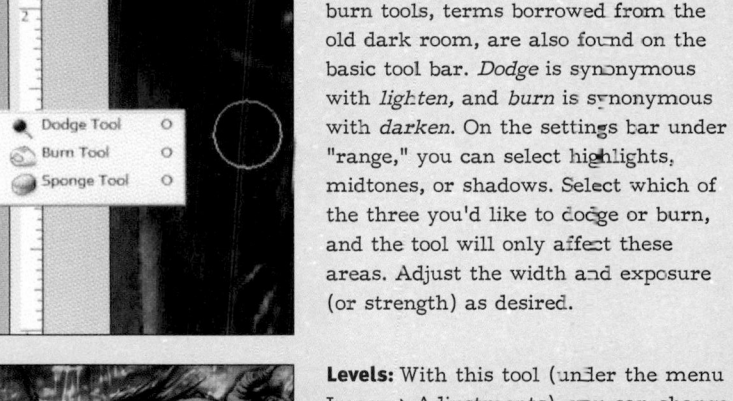

Dodge and Burn Tools: The dodge and burn tools, terms borrowed from the old dark room, are also found on the basic tool bar. *Dodge* is synonymous with *lighten,* and *burn* is synonymous with *darken.* On the settings bar under "range," you can select highlights, midtones, or shadows. Select which of the three you'd like to dodge or burn, and the tool will only affect these areas. Adjust the width and exposure (or strength) as desired.

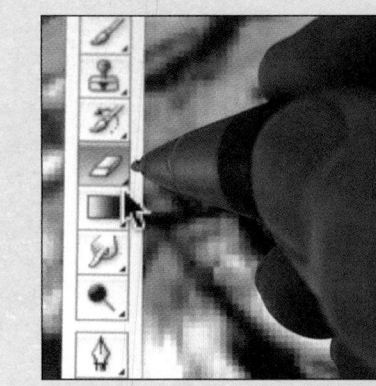

Paintbrush Tool: The paintbrush tool, on the basic tool bar in Photoshop®, allows you to apply layers of color to your canvas. Like the eraser, dodge, and burn tools, you can adjust the diameter and opacity of the brush to control the width and strength of your strokes.

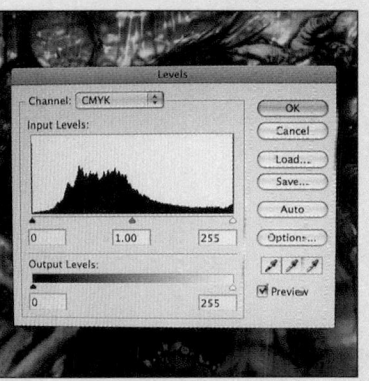

Levels: With this tool (under the menu Image > Adjustments), you can change the brightness, contrast, and range of values within an image. The black, midtone, and white of the image are represented by the three markers along the bottom of the graph. Slide these markers horizontally. Moving the black marker right will darken the overall image, moving the white marker left will lighten the overall image, and sliding the midtone marker left or right will bring the midtones darker or lighter, respectively.

Color Picker: Choose the color of your "paint" in the color picker window. Select your hue by clicking within the vertical color bar; then move the circular cursor around the box to change the color's tone.

107

Vampire Queen

This beautiful and deadly vampire queen inhabits the castle in the Vampire Slayer illustration on page 24. With each kill she makes, she adds another drop of blood to her tattoo—a constant reminder of the hunger that drives her. Inspired by anime illustrations, this character should look sexy and cute—but a bit dangerous too.

Materials
- Vellum paper
- Eraser
- Black colored pencil
- Tracing paper
- Photoshop®

▲ **Step One** Create a thumbnail illustration with a thumbnail drawn on a sheet of tracing paper with a black colored pencil.

◄ **Step Two** Once you're happy with the rough sketch, begin the final drawing on vellum paper, still using the black colored pencil. This will be a classic composition where the main character takes up 90% of the image with a hint of the environment behind her. (You may choose to transfer this sketch; see "Transferring a Drawing" on page 25.)

108

Step Three Next, start working on her facial features. Soften the arch of her eyebrow a bit — most anime characters tend to have a vulnerable, innocent expression. Keep her eyes large, with her nose and mouth tiny in comparison.

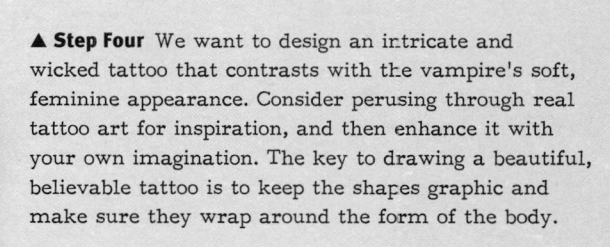

▲ **Step Four** We want to design an intricate and wicked tattoo that contrasts with the vampire's soft, feminine appearance. Consider perusing through real tattoo art for inspiration, and then enhance it with your own imagination. The key to drawing a beautiful, believable tattoo is to keep the shapes graphic and make sure they wrap around the form of the body.

◄ **Step Five** In this step, we'll shade in her thick black hair, keeping it whimsical and luxurious. Using an eraser, pick out the glowing highlights cast from the moon. Outline parts of her hair for a slight cartoonish look, but then go over it with a soft edge to stay true to the texture of hair.

◀ **Step Six** Now, add more drops of blood and thorny edges to her tattoo. Remember the story behind her tattoo — how she adds a new drop of blood with each kill. Use both soft and hard lines so the design will look three-dimensional on her arm. Indicate some lace embroidery on the upper edge of her bodice.

▶ **Step Seven** Begin darkening all the values in her hair, skin, and dress. Give her skin a light tone, using a cool 30% gray colored pencil; then you can pick out highlights with an eraser. Use firm-edged core shadows on her bodice to indicate the sheen of a silky fabric. We want a romantic, wind-swept quality for the border treatment, making our vampire look almost like an apparition. Use the waves in her hair as inspiration and incorporate soft, sweeping lines into the frame.

Step Eight We did a full rendering of the vampire queen's castle in the Vampire Slayer illustration (see page 24). Since these two characters are from the same story, let's bring the castle into this background as well. To save time, scan both drawings into Photoshop®; then crop out the castle and place it into this illustration.

▶ **Step Ten** Now we'll begin the color stage. Start with her skin tone and select a light peachy pink from the color picker. Then, choose the brush tool and turn the opacity down to about 10%. Bring the hardness of the brush down as well. Select the "multiply" mode so you have more control over the saturation — this allows the drawing to come through. Continue brushing over her skin until you get the desired effect. Repeat these steps for the hair and dress.

Step Twelve Since this vampire is royalty, we want her status reflected in her clothes. Choose hot pink for the light areas of her dress. Bright spots of color next to deep core shadows will give the impression of a luxurious velvet material. Select a deep orange-yellow for the gold embroidery. Then, with the eraser tool set at medium opacity, run a highlight down the middle.

Step Thirteen Anime characters are known for enormous, limpid eyes. With the eraser tool, give your vampire queen small, bright highlights in the pupil and along the bottom rim. Also, give her eye a color that will contrast nicely with her hair.

113

▲ Step Fourteen We don't want the saturated blue of her hair to look foreign to the rest of our vampire, so we're going to bring a bit of this color into her skin tone. Take some of the blue, keep the opacity of the brush tool extremely low, and bring it into her eyes, into the bottom plane of the nose, and into all the shadow areas.

◄ Step Fifteen Next, we're going to use the brush tool again while we work on the blood and lips. Increase the opacity to about 70% and add smatterings of dark red along the side of her mouth.

◄ Step Sixteen
Give the background a tint of turquoise blue. We're not going to do too much more to it since it's supposed to be a second read.

▲ Step Seventeen Using the brush tool, start adding color to her tattoo. Select a brighter red, different from the blood on her chin.

◄ Step Eighteen Now you're going to tie the illustration together by bringing colors from the eye and dress into the tattoo. Use muted gold, green, and gray to contrast with the bright splashes of red.

115

Step Nineteen Since tattoos are known for their graphic design, we're going to finish off the tattoo by outlining all the shapes with a darker holding line. At this point, I add a bit of fun by creating a rainbow that bursts out of the sword.

▲ **Step Twenty** Now we're going to add more peach tones into her skin. Keep your brush tool on multiply mode and select a warm, off-white color from the palette. Then, brighten all the light areas on her face and chest. Bring in soft, warm violet hues for the shadow areas, such as underneath her nose and chin.

◄ **Step Twenty-One** Even though the background is a second read, we still want to give it some life. Use the brush tool and choose a vibrant green for the moon and the bats. We don't want to leave the background completely cool, however, so select a burnt umber and use it to paint parts of the castle. Then, with the eraser tool, add thin, squiggly rings around the moon. This suggests supernatural electrical current pulses radiating from the castle.

Step Twenty-Two For the final step, use the same green to highlight the edges around her hair. Also use a little bit of this color to frame the whole picture. At this point, you'll see that I changed the hot pink color of her dress to a deep elegant red, which better mimics the look of fine velvet.

Vampires in our Culture

The timeline below shows how our view of the vampire has changed over the past hundred years, transforming him from dreaded monster to civil rights victim to teenage heartthrob. Still hunted after all these years, the vampire is rarely spotted anymore in his natural habitat of Romania or Transylvania. However, he can certainly be found in many movies, television series, and young adult novels.

1813: The Giaour
Poem written by Lord Byron

Inspired by his many travels throughout the Middle East and Europe, Lord Byron's poem combines the Eastern European vampire legends with the Turkish practice of drowning a woman guilty of an affair with an infidel. As punishment, the *giaour*—or infidel—in this story was destined to become a vampire who would then feed on his loved ones.

1819: The Vampyre
Short story written by John Polidori

At first credited to Lord Byron, this story by John Polidori tells the adventures of Lord Ruthven, a vampire who mysteriously drains the life from the women he meets. This tale was a turning point in the ancient vampire legends and the first time one of the undead was portrayed as a charismatic and seductive aristocrat. Polidori based his character on the exploits of his one-time friend, Lord Byron.

1897: Dracula
Book written by Bram Stoker

Influenced by Polidori's *The Vampyre* and inspired by tales of Vlad Dracula of Walachia, this vampire novel is mainly told through letters and journal entries, as well as newspaper snippets. This is the first time we meet the legendary Count Dracula, his vampire brides, and Van Helsing. In 25 years, this book would be retold in the new media of moving pictures in the film *Nosferatu*.

1922: Nosferatu
Film directed by F. W. Murnau

Filmed in black and white, this silent German horror film changed the names of all the characters in the classic tale because the studio didn't have the rights to Bram Stoker's novel. It's still one of the best and scariest cinematic portrayals of Dracula to date.

1931: Dracula
Film directed by Tod Browning

Béla Lugosi plays the leading role in this film based on Bram Stoker's distinguished novel. As Count Dracula, Lugosi changes from a bat to a vampire, hypnotizes his victims, and feeds upon the unsuspecting Lucy Weston.

1954: I Am Legend
Book written by Richard Matheson

A ground-breaking story, this novel was the first to incorporate elements of a vampire plague and a subsequent worldwide apocalypse. This book was made into film at least three times: *The Last Man on Earth* (1964); *The Omega Man* (1971); and *I Am Legend* (2007). Matheson's vampire tale also inspired director George A. Romero's *Night of the Living Dead,* and thus became the progenitor of subsequent zombie stories.

1954: The Vampira Show
TV series directed by Hap Weyman

Played by Maila Nurmi, who in turn drew inspiration from Charles Addams' *New Yorker* cartoons, the character of Vampira combined elegance with horror. With her long fingernails and even longer cigarette holder, she sauntered through a bank of fog, and then screamed before introducing the movie of the evening. This show later morphed in 1982 to become *Elvira's Movie Macabre.*

1964: The Munsters
TV series created by Allan Burns and Chris Hayward

This half-hour comedy aired on CBS for two seasons. Starring Fred Gwyne as a Frankenstein monster named Hermon and Yvonne De Carlo as the sultry Lily, this sitcom portrayed everyday life within a family of ghouls. With no overt depiction of vampires, De Carlo definitely looked the part of a life-draining enchantress, while Grandpa was later revealed as Count (Sam) Dracula.

1966: Dark Shadows
TV series created by Dan Curtis

Starring Jonathan Frid as the vampire Barnabas Collins, this ABC gothic soap opera was filmed in a castle-like mansion. The setting helped to create the moody and romantic ambiance that became a trademark for the series. The show also featured ghosts, werewolves, time travel, witches, and on occasion, an alternate universe. Fans of the show include Johnny Dep, Tim Burton, and Madonna.

1975: Salem's Lot
Book written by Stephen King

Like all of King's books, this story hooks the reader from beginning to end. Main character Ben Mears moves home after the death of his wife. Before long, Mears begins to suspect that the strange deaths and disappearances that take place in Jerusalem's Lot are the handiwork of vampires.

1976: Interview with the Vampire
Book written by Anne Rice

Once a plantation owner and now a tormented vampire, Louis tells the story of his 200-year life to a journalist. He details his relationships with Lestat, the vampire who turned him, and Claudia, a vampire forever trapped in a child's body, and reveals the secret world of Parisian vampires. The first in *The Vampire Chronicles* series, this book subsequently became a movie in 1994, starring Tom Cruise and Brad Pitt.

1983: The Hunger
Film directed by Tony Scott

Catherine Deneuve stars as an immortal vampire with David Bowie as her lover and fellow blood-sucker. Susan Sarandon enters the picture as a doctor trying to help Bowie, who is aging rapidly. The plot takes a chilling twist when Deneuve seduces Sarandon and invites her to partake in eternal life.

1987: The Lost Boys
Film directed by Joel Schumacher

Starring Jason Patrick, Corey Haim, and Keifer Sutherland, this horror classic focuses on an infestation of teenage vampires in a sleepy little California town. The temptation of supernatural powers, eternal life, and forbidden love lure Patrick toward a coven of local vampires who want him to join them.

1991: The Vampire Diaries
Book written by L. J. Smith

Published in 1991, this young adult series currently contains seven books. Featuring a high school girl named Elena Gilbert, the story focuses on her conflicting emotions toward two vampiric brothers, Stefan and Damon. In 2009, this popular book series was made into a television series on the CW Network. Starring Ian Somerhalder as Damon and Paul Wesley as Stefan, the show became an almost overnight hit.

1992: Bram Stoker's Dracula
Film directed by Francis Ford Coppola

Genres blend in this horror-romance-thriller that stars Gary Oldman as Dracula and Winona Ryder as Mina Harker. This retelling of the classic tale focuses on the suicide of Dracula's wife, her reincarnation in Mina, and the subsequent vampire triangle that ensues.

1993: Guilty Pleasures
Book written by Laurell K. Hamilton

In this first novel in the series, readers are introduced to Anita Blake, a vampire hunter who lives in an alternate history. Blake's world is filled with werewolves, vampires, and magic, and the story is written with elements of detective fiction and the supernatural. The series currently contains 19 novels.

1996: From Dusk Till Dawn
Film directed by Robert Rodriguez

Acting as bank robbers, George Clooney and Quentin Tarantino encounter a coven of vampires in a Mexican strip club. There, they battle for their lives from dusk until dawn.

1998: Blade
Film directed by Stephen Norrington

Based on a character in the Marvel Comics, Wesley Snipes portrays Blade — a half-vampire, half-human hybrid who hunts vampires. This character is most likely based on ancient Balkan legends of the dhamphir. The film was followed by *Elade II* in 2002, a film directed by Guillermo del Toro.

1999: Buffy the Vampire Slayer
TV series created by Joss Whedon

This cult favorite starred Sarah Michelle Gellar as Buffy Sommers, self-proclaimed vampire hunter and high school student. In between classes, Sommers regularly stalked and staked the undead. The TV series *Angel* was a spin-off from this show.

2001: The Southern Vampire Mysteries
Books written by Charlaine Harris

Set in an alternate history, this series of books stars Sookie Stackhouse and takes place in Louisiana. Werewolves, shape shifters, fairies, and vampires are part of the everday fabric of Stackhouse's small town, where she works as a barmaid. A key element in the series is the depiction of the vampire as a creature still denied civil rights in some countries. In 2008, the *True Blood* series began on HBO. Created by Alan Ball and based on the book series by Charlaine Harris, the show has already won an Emmy and a Golden Globe.

2003: Underworld
Film directed by Len Wiseman

Starring Kate Beckinsale, this gothic film series features both vampires and werewolves. Putting a plot spin on the classic vampire hunter, the main character, Selene, is a vampire who hunts and kills werewolves. Followed by the 2006 film *Underworld: Evolution* directed by Len Wiseman, and the 2009 film *Underworld: Rise of the Lycans* directed by Patrick Tatopoulos.

2004: Van Helsing
Film directed by Stephen Sommers

With Hugh Jackman playing a legendary monster hunter and Kate Beckinsale as a member of a cursed Transylvanian family, this gothic film shows glimpses of Frankenstein's monster, Dr. Jekyll and Mr. Hyde, and a werewolf, before focusing on the real monster of the day: Count Dracula.

2005: Twilight
Book by Stephanie Meyer

This young-adult novel tells the epic tale of a 17-year-old girl, Bella, who falls in love with what appears to be a 17-year-old boy, but turns out to be a 104-year-old vampire named Edward Cullen. The plot thickens when the town of Forks is invaded by a rival vampire coven. The series includes the novels *New Moon, Eclipse,* and *Breaking Dawn. Twilight* the movie was released in 2008, further cementing this series in the hearts of teens worldwide.

Vampire Flyer

Considered one of the most dangerous predators, this vampire—who can shape shift into a flying winged monster—was captured and chained in the midst of his transformation. Bearing wounds from previous battles like trophies, this warrior knows that the humans won't have the upper hand for long.

Materials

- Acrylic paints: Alizarin crimson, raw sienna, yellow ochre, ultramarine blue, burnt umber
- Palette box
- Matte medium
- White gesso
- Old house painting brush
- Masonite board
- Assortment of small acrylic paintbrushes
- Tracing paper
- Vellum paper
- Black colored pencil
- White colored pencil
- Eraser
- Photoshop®

▲ **Step One** For this project, we'll be making a portrait of a flying vampire. To begin our drawing, we'll start off by creating a thumbnail on a sheet of tracing paper, using a black colored pencil. Rough out his body and the position of his wings.

▶ **Step Two** Next, we'll begin the final drawing. We want his wings to be even more imposing, so bring his body down in size. With your basic outline in place, start with your dark shadow values first and shade in his beard, hair, and eye sockets. There will be so much detail to come that we want to keep certain areas like these as dark, graphic shapes. (You may choose to transfer this sketch; see "Transferring a Drawing" on page 25.)

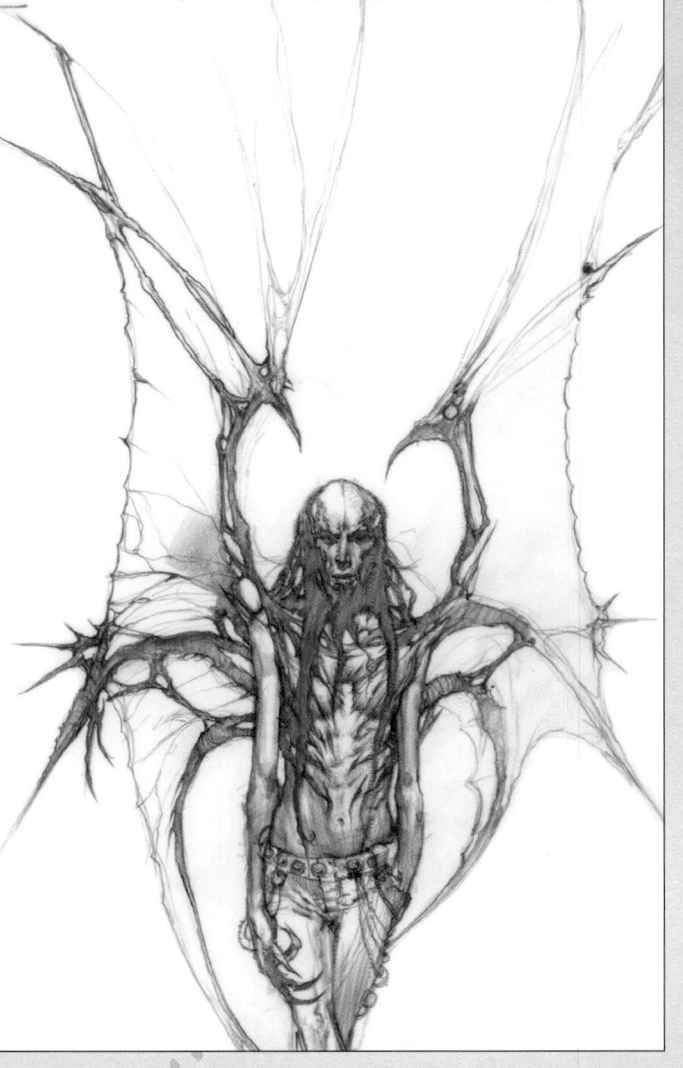

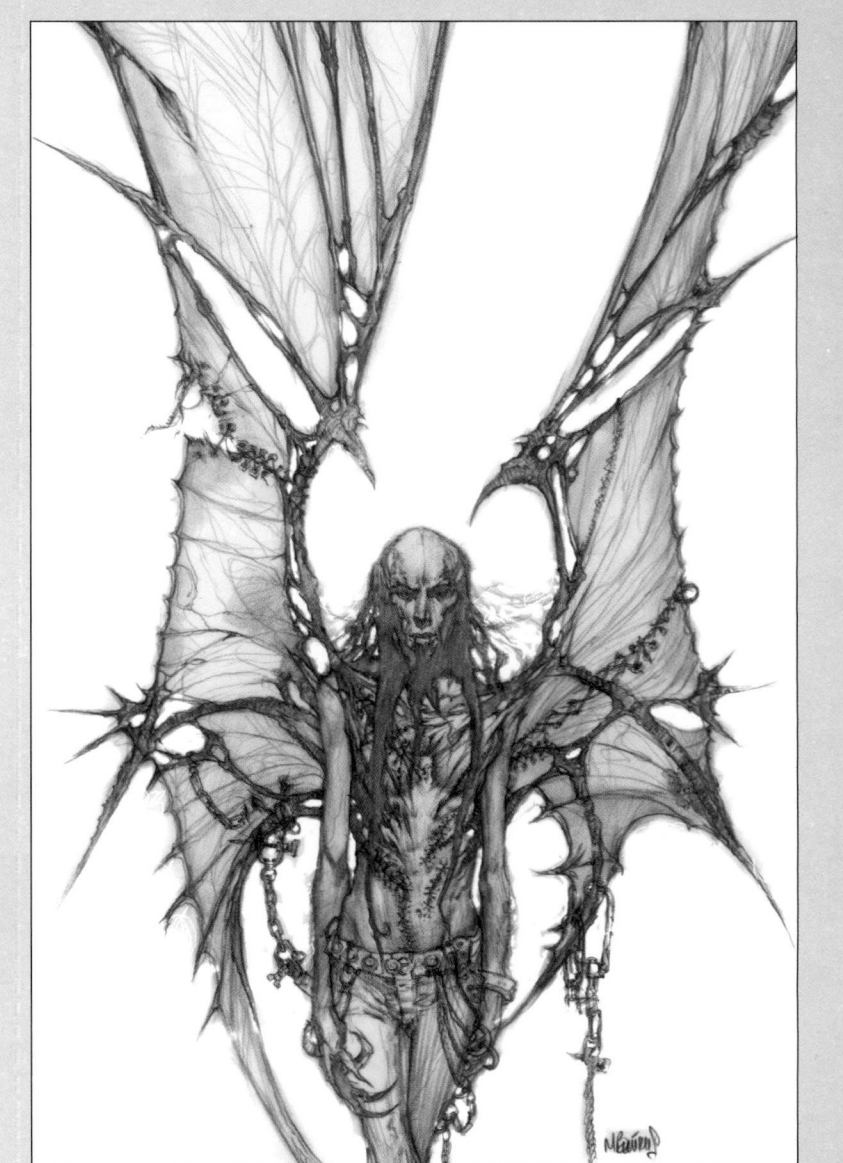

◄ Step Three Using the side of your pencil, begin to chisel out the vampire's anatomy. Keep your pencil strokes long and clean to accentuate his emaciated body. We want his wings to look intimidating and fragile at the same time. Notice the razor-sharp thorns jutting out from the sides that hold the membrane-like skin together.

► Step Four Darken the whole figure using the side of your pencil. Vary the values slightly on the skin of the wings to keep them looking transparent. Then, go over all the edges with a soft value to lend more realism to the drawing. In this step, you'll also add the chains his captors have put on him. Since they are made up of thick rope, silver, and bolts, he has thankfully remained incapacitated. Well, for the time being at least.

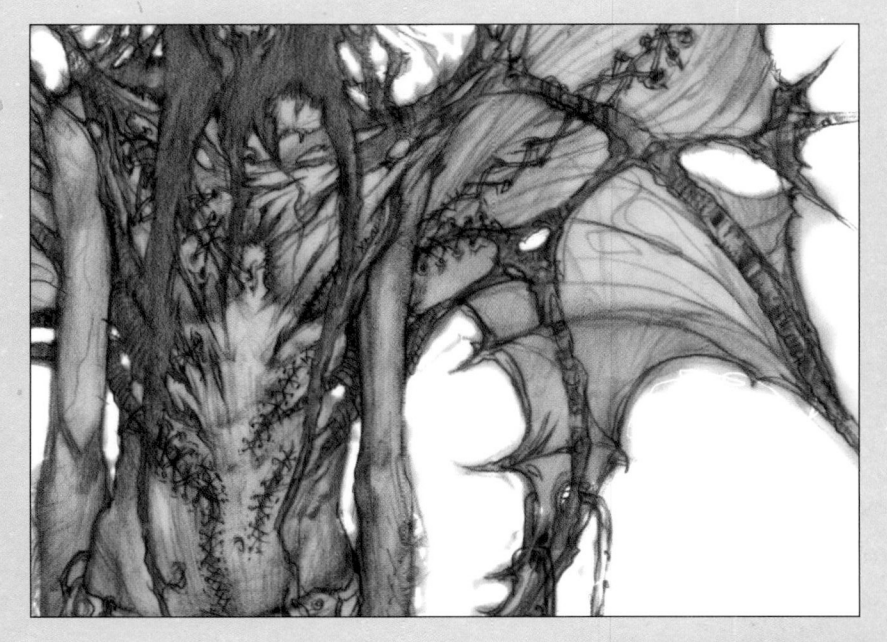

◄ Step Five Wounded during numerous battles with humans, this vampire has had his wings stitched up more than once. Indicate the stitches using uneven "X" patterns and punctuate them with small, dark holes. Make sure to keep a slight curve on each "X" so they conform to his musculature.

121

122

◀ **Step Six** Now, make a duplicate of the drawing on a copy machine using standard copy paper. Using the available options on the machine, adjust the value by darkening it 20%. This immediately gives you the mid value you want for the background. Now you are ready to paint. Note: Using a copy machine is entirely optional. You can achieve the same effect by painting a semi-transparent gray tone to the image once you've mounted and spray-fixed it onto the board. You might also choose to begin the drawing on gray-toned paper or TV gray paper.

▶ **Step Seven** Now we can have a little more fun with the drawing. On the copy you've made, take a white colored pencil and add some bright highlights down his chest, on his wings, and the top of his head. Also add some long, fuzzy hair around his forearms.

▼ **Step Eight** At this point, let's see how the drawing will look in red tones. First, scan it into Photoshop® and adjust the color balance to a warm value. This will make it much easier to achieve the colors we want. Print out a copy. Then, mount it onto a masonite board by brushing it with a mixture of 50% matte medium and 50% water. This seals the copy and allows you to paint over it.

◄ Step Ten Mix warm and cool washes of paint, then allow them to "pool" in certain areas of the wings. This will give them a thin, transparent look. Then, dilute some white gesso with water and use a fine-tip brush to paint striations along the wing. Use the same mixture to lightly brush a highlight down the middle of each wing to create dimension and form.

▲ Step Nine Use a mixture of yellow ochre, ultramarine blue, alizarin crimson, and good deal of water for the vampire's skin. You only need to use light washes of color since you'll be allowing the red tones of the print to show through. Leave the large shadow areas. They have nice graphic shapes and add a sense of mystery to the piece.

► Step Eleven Next, we want to emphasize how the vampire's skin stretches and pulls over his emaciated form. Take your diluted gesso mixture and use a small brush to paint thin strips across his cranium and chest. To make the shadows along his sternum and ribcage recede even further, use a cool mixture of ultramarine blue with a bit of yellow ochre.

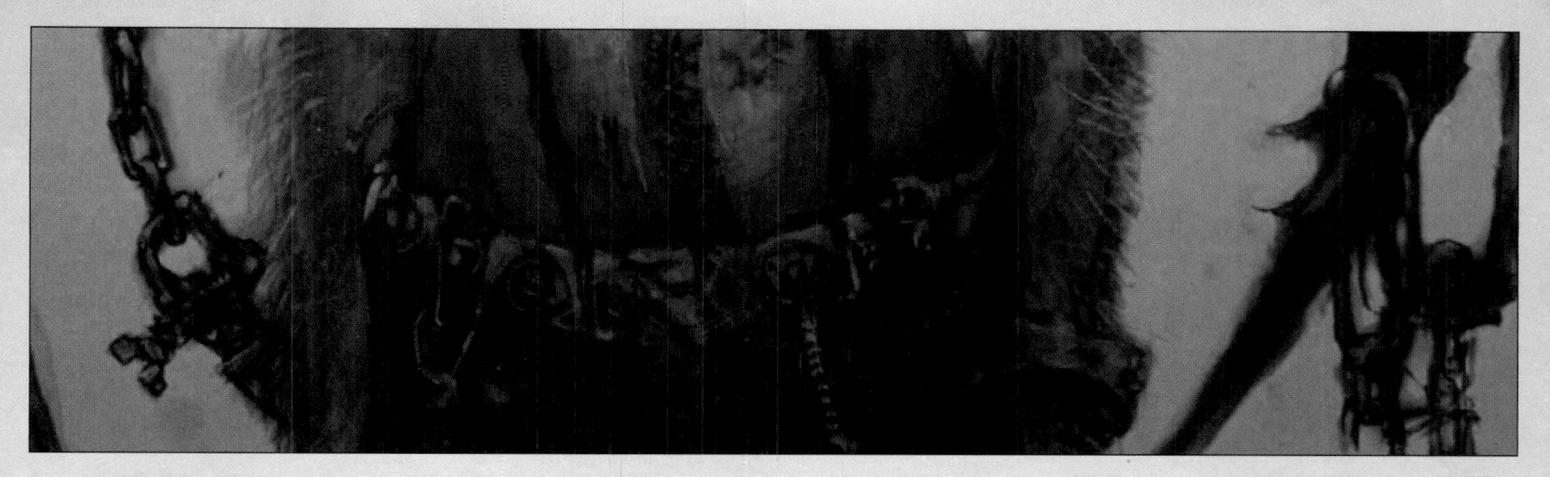

Step Twelve To create the silver chains and buckles, add a little ultramarine blue to the gesso mixture. Then use this to paint the metal forms, leaving the shadows untouched.

◄ **Step Thirteen** Now scan your painting back into Photoshop® for the finishing touches. By using Photoshop® for the last stage, you can finish the illustration much more quickly and have room for experimentation.

Step Fourteen Here's where experimentation pays off. Out of curiosity, I started to adjust the color balance and found that I liked this cooler, muted version. These colors seem more appropriate for the creepy vampire's undead status.

Step Fifteen Select the eraser tool to brighten the highlights on the silver metal and the vampire's chest. Set the opacity to about 50% and decrease the diameter of the brush accordingly.

▶ **Step Sixteen** For the final step, we're going to create a smoky background for our vampire. This will allow the viewer to mentally write their own the story for this image. First, select the dodge tool. Then, set the opacity to about 10% and the hardness to 20%. Use the tool to design swirls of smoke that waft around him. Then, increase the opacity by another 10%, and add some highlights within the smoke to give it dimension.

DETAILS

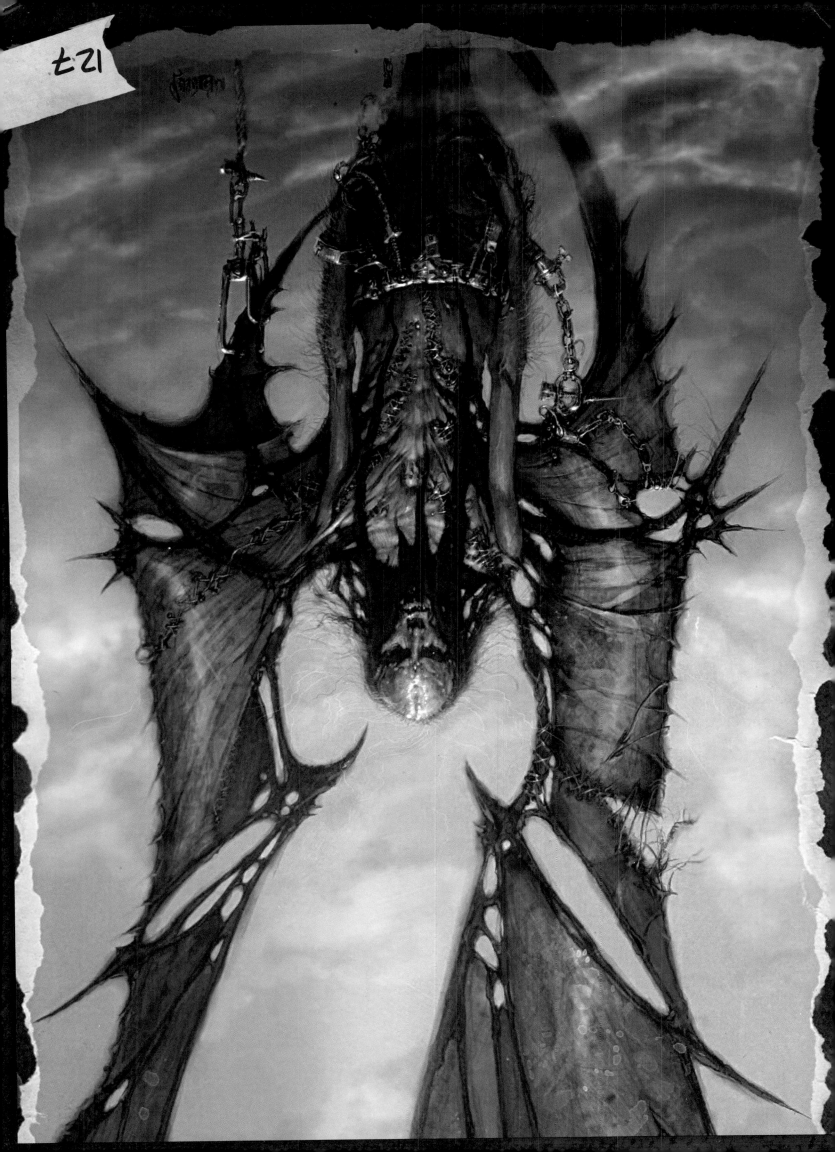

The Legend Continues

Hail, brave soul! Despite the rough terrain of fang and claw, you've resisted the Fantasy Underground's most charismatic monster: the vampire. As part of your ultimate survival test, you've learned how to draw an entire flock of vampires and their enemies, from an alluring bounty hunter to an insatiable glutton to a vampire queen. Your daring accomplishments now include oil and acrylic painting, pencil illustration, and computer manipulation. The tables have been turned and now the prey has become the predator. You need no longer fear the terror of this blood-sucking beast, for if you have successfully completed your mission and the projects in this book, then you are now as legendary as Van Helsing himself. Hearty cheers for the new Vampire Master! May your reign over the immortals continue until your next journey into the Fantasy Underground.

Meet the Authors

Mike Butkus

Mike Butkus, one of the top entertainment illustrators and conceptual artists since 1990, has been involved in the advertising, production, art direction, character development and set design for more than 2,500 film and television series. During the last ten years, Mike has been able to unleash his twisted imagination on the rising gaming industry, designing and illustrating fantastic creatures, characters, and environments for all the interactive players to enjoy. To see Mike's own personal work, which is now available for merchandising and licensing, visit www.offleashconceptart.com or www.mikebutkus.net.

Merrie Destefano

Merrie Destefano left a 9-to-5 desk job to become a full-time freelance editor and novelist, writing science fiction and fantasy. With 20 years' experience in publishing, her background ranges from award-winning graphic designer and illustrator to editor of *Victorian Homes* magazine and founding editor of *Cottages & Bungalows* magazine. She currently lives in Southern California with her husband, their German shepherds, a Siamese cat, and the occasional wandering possum. For more information, visit www.merriedestefano.com.